I0099131

THE RIGHTEOUSNESS OF GOD
Challenges and Illumination

Daniel Mann

THE
RIGHTEOUSNESS
OF GOD

Challenges and Illumination

Daniel Mann

THE RIGHTEOUSNESS OF GOD
Challenges and Illumination
© 2022 by Daniel Mann

All rights reserved.
Written permission must be secured from the author to use or reproduce any part of this book, except for brief quotations in critical reviews or articles.

Printed in the United States of America

Unless otherwise indicated,
Scripture quotations are from:

The Holy Bible, English Standard Version® (ESV)
© 2001 by Crossway,
a publishing ministry of Good News Publishers.
All rights reserved.

Other Scripture quotations:

The Holy Bible, American Standard Version (ASV)
© 1901 by Thomas Nelson & Sons
Public domain.

The Holy Bible, King James Version (KJV)
© 2011 by Barbour Publishing, Inc.
All rights reserved.

Holy Bible, New American Standard Bible® (NASB)
© 1960, 1962, 1963, 1971, 1972, 1973, 1975, 1977, 1995
by The Lockman Foundation.
All rights reserved.

The Holy Bible, The New International Version® (NIV)
© 1973, 1978, 1984 by International Bible Society.
All rights reserved.

Holy Bible, New Living Translation® (NLT)
© 1996, 2004, 2015 by Tyndale House Foundation.
All rights reserved.

Front cover photo by Daniel Mann
Author photo by Anita Mann

Daniel Mann, author
Van Misheff, editor

Other books by Daniel Mann, *edited by* Van Misheff

PRAYER: *Confronting the Confusion*
THEOLOGY: *Reclaiming the Relevance*
SCRIPTURE: *Quest for Understanding*
THE GOD OF THE BIBLE: *Logical, Evidential, Historical Proofs*

ॐ

Contents

God and Evil

Acknowledgments

I would like to express appreciation to those who helped support me along the way in writing this book.

My faithful wife, Anita, has been a support to me in so many ways—through her encouragement, and through her prayers and spiritual backing. She also provides for my personal needs which enable me to devote myself to writing and teaching. Without this support, I would have been overwhelmed by daily material concerns.

I would also like to express my gratitude for my friend, Rob Thomas, who used his valuable time to offer his insightful commentary on every chapter of the book. In addition, he has provided much-appreciated spiritual encouragement throughout the process.

Last but not least, I want to acknowledge, with special gratitude and appreciation, my seminary buddy and dear friend, Van Misheff, who is the Editor of this book and four of my previous books. I think that Van has worked harder on my books than I have. He graciously describes his editing as "polishing the gold," but Van has also offered great support and encouragement throughout this whole endeavor. His standard of excellence is invaluable.

Above all, I must thank my Savior and Lord, Jesus Christ, who has called me to continually search out His Word, meditating on it day and night. I am indebted to the Holy Spirit's guidance and inspiration throughout the entire writing process. It has been a great privilege and blessing to Me, as I seek to glorify Him in all I write, say and do.

Daniel Mann

THE RIGHTEOUSNESS OF GOD

This book is a defense of God's righteousness, an attempt to neutralize the charges against the God of the Bible. The atheist, Richard Dawkins, had written:

> The God of the Old Testament is arguably the most un-pleasant character in all fiction: jealous and proud of it; a petty, unjust, unforgiving control-freak; a vindictive, bloodthirsty ethnic cleanser; a misogynistic, homophobic, racist, infanticidal, genocidal, filicidal, pestilential, megalo-maniacal, sadomasochistic, capriciously malevolent bully.[1]

Is Dawkins correct? While it is true that God punishes, He does so with great patience. As He explained to Abraham, He would wait several hundred years before punishing the Canaanites for their numerous moral abominations, including the sacrifice of their children to their gods. Likewise, God waited hundreds of years before He brought judgment upon Judah through the Babylonians:

> The LORD, the God of their fathers, sent persistently to them by his messengers, because he had compassion on his people and on his dwelling place. But they kept mocking the messengers of God, despising his words and scoffing at his prophets, until the wrath of the LORD rose against his people, until there was no remedy.
>
> 2 CHRONICLES 36:15–16

Does the righteous God not have a right to judge His creation? Wouldn't a world without judgment prove to be worse? Some skeptics are convinced that if there is *any* suffering, punishment, or death, it proves that God is unrighteous. They argue that if God is omnipotent, He should have been able to design a pain-free, death-free world. However, without considering eternity, the skeptic finds it easy to fault everything.

Perhaps we need to experience pain. Perhaps there are prohibitive, hidden costs that accrue when we don't experience pain. For example, a leper cannot experience pain. This might sound like a good state of being at first glance. However, without the sensation of pain, lepers can injure their bodies, grievously. Similarly, perhaps there are many other hidden costs associated with the absence of pain which we are unable to weigh or even to perceive. Such considerations make judging God and His plan nearly impossible.

A month or two after their great deliverance through the waters of the Red Sea, the Israelites were thirsty, with no water available (Exodus 17). Surely, this represented a betrayal by God, right? The Israelites complained that God had brought them out of Egypt but would abandon them to die in the wilderness. Therefore, Israel rebelled against Moses and wrongly judged the Lord. Why would they do this? There were several things they could not see, apart from the eyes of faith:

1. They could not know that their thirst would soon be satisfied by a river of water emanating from a rock.

2. They did not know that God had good reasons to humble them:

   > "And he humbled you and let you hunger and fed you with manna, which you did not know, nor did your fathers know, that he might make you know that man does not live by bread alone, but man lives by every word that comes from the mouth of the LORD."
   >
   > DEUTERONOMY 8:3

3. They needed to learn to trust God by abiding in His Word, rather than relying on their own "wisdom."

4. They could not appreciate the eternal value and implications of these lessons.

When we are near-sighted, it is easy to find fault.

~

The challenges against the righteousness of God are numerous. The objections come, not only from the outside, but also from within the Church and even from the Bible. I too have often been challenged when I would read verses like these:

> The coming of the lawless one is by the activity of Satan with all power and false signs and wonders, and with all wicked deception for those who are perishing, because they refused to love the truth and so be saved. Therefore God sends them a strong delusion, so that they may believe what is false, in order that all may be condemned who did not believe the truth but had pleasure in unrighteousness.
>
> 2 THESSALONIANS 2:9–12

Such a passage raises many difficult questions:

- *Why did God create Satan, and why does He allow him to persist?*
- *Why does God even participate in the work of Satan by sending those who are perishing a "strong delusion?" Shouldn't He instead send them the truth of the Gospel?*

These are difficult questions, and here's another:

- *If God saved an unworthy like me, then why doesn't He regenerate every heart so that we all might believe?*

How do we answer such questions? I began to wonder if these questions have plagued other Christians. Some admit that they aren't particularly concerned. They just know what they have seen and experienced; therefore, they could easily set these questions aside. I have never been able to do this. Although I tried to banish these questions into the darkest crevasses of my mind, they would creep out to pester me, like mosquitoes at night. They were masters of torment, forcing me to confront them head-on.

Therefore, I wondered whether writing on this subject would be of help to others. Over the course of many years of posting my essays on social media, I have noticed that few have the time—or inclination—to read such essays.

So then, why should I continue? For one thing, answering these perplexing questions, at least tentatively, has enabled me to stand and to approach my Savior with confidence and joy:

> Therefore, brothers, since we have confidence to enter the holy places by the blood of Jesus, by the new and living way that he opened for us through the curtain, that is, through his flesh, and since we have a great priest over the house of God, let us draw near with a true heart in full assurance of faith, with our hearts sprinkled clean from an evil conscience and our bodies washed with pure water. Let us hold fast the confession of our hope without wavering, for he who promised is faithful.
>
> HEBREWS 10:19–23

The Lord did not simply snap His fingers and then, by some sort of holy magic, I was instantaneously given assurance. Instead, He led me to meditate on His Word day and night, according to Psalm 1:1-3 and Joshua 1:8. Over time, the answers I was seeking came together, through the agency of the Holy Spirit, to comfort me with His peace and assurance.

However, let me be the first to admit: I have not obtained comprehensive answers. In many cases, I don't think we are presently capable of such fullness of understanding. There are too many blanks that need to be filled. Instead, according to 1 Corinthians 13:12, we are cautioned that we can only partially understand God's revelation to us. Yet, I have found that even a partial understanding has proven to be a delight of enduring riches. The Apostle Paul had labored for this very purpose:

> … that their hearts may be encouraged, being knit together in love, to reach all the riches of full assurance of understanding and the knowledge of God's mystery, which is Christ, in whom are hidden all the treasures of wisdom and knowledge.
>
> COLOSSIANS 2:2–3

We are vulnerable and lack confidence because we do not meditate on the Word as we should. Consequently, we cannot stand against the challenges to our faith. Much of the time, we are not even aware of what those challenges are. Paul was concerned as well about this issue:

> I say this in order that no one may delude you with plausible arguments.
>
> COLOSSIANS 2:4

The plausible arguments against the faith of which Paul spoke have proliferated on a global scale. The Church has been withering before the assaults of biblical criticism, multiculturalism, Darwinism, and moral relativism. To cite just one consequence, most churchgoers now believe that there are many roads to salvation.

If we believe just this one heresy, what will happen to evangelism and our zeal for the Bible? We will become fair-game for the latest deceptive message. Our confidence in the Gospel of Christ will wither like grass with no rain.

∼

This book is essentially a defense of the righteousness of God and the Christian faith. However, many will retort: "God doesn't need a defense. Rather, He is quite able to defend Himself." While this is true, it is also true that our Lord wants us to follow Him, even in His footsteps:

> If we live by the Spirit, let us also keep in step with the Spirit.
>
> GALATIANS 5:25

To do this is not arrogant or presumptuous. In fact, it is what He expects us to do. He calls us to make a defense for the Faith, the Faith that He bought for us on the Cross:

> Beloved, although I was very eager to write to you about our common salvation, I found it necessary to write appealing to you to contend for the faith that was once for all delivered to the saints.
>
> JUDE 3

When we contend for the Faith, we are essentially contending for God—for His ways, His deeds, and His promises:

> ... but in your hearts honor Christ the Lord as holy, always being prepared to make a defense to anyone who asks you for a reason for the hope that is in you; yet do it with gentleness and respect. ...
>
> 1 PETER 3:15

We honor our Lord by making a defense for the Hope we have and for the Word He has given us. By His mercies, this is what this book intends to do. My prayer is that I might be able to provide answers so that my brethren might live their lives in Christ with confidence and zeal.

*

The Problem of Suffering

CHAPTER 1

Is Suffering and Pain Evidence of God's Injustice?

If God is all-powerful and all-loving, why is there so much suffering? This is a massive question and can be approached from many different directions. As with all of our *"Why did God"* questions, we cannot answer this one comprehensively, but perhaps we can offer some meaningful answers.

Why is there so much suffering?

Perhaps we need it. I know that I do. Suffering teaches us and helps us grow. Without suffering, we tend to take our closest relationships for granted. A woman I knew faithfully nursed her husband through his nine-year struggle with cancer. Over the course of his ordeal, the husband came to truly love his wife.

Captured on video following a catastrophic Haitian earthquake, a husband could be seen crying and fervently kissing his wife. She had been dug out of the rubble—alive—several days after the quake. Suffering and loss teach us to value what we have. That is why the psalmist wrote about our need to be aware of our impending death:

> So teach us to number our days that we may get a heart of wisdom.
>
> PSALM 90:12

We need to be reminded of painful consequences—especially the inevitability of death—to provoke us to seek wisdom. Furthermore, King David suggested that the awareness of our temporary sojourn through life might also be a means by which we can learn humility:

"O LORD, make me know my end and what is the measure of my days; let me know how fleeting I am! Behold, you have made my days a few handbreadths, and my lifetime is as nothing before you. Surely all mankind stands as a mere breath! Surely a man goes about as a shadow!"

PSALM 39:4–6A

It is humbling to realize that we will die. Everything we have worked for will come to an end. While a man struggles to exalt himself and to prove his significance, it all amounts to nothing after his last breath.

It is our suffering and neediness that draws us together.

When things are going too well for us, we tend to become jaded, self-satisfied, and arrogant.

Why are we afflicted with the likes of mosquitoes, birth pains, or cancer? Could it be that we need them? Perhaps the curses enumerated in Genesis 3:14-19 were a blessing in disguise! What could I possibly mean by such a claim? For just one example among many, consider this: grooming is both the glue and the very substance of baboon society. It is through grooming that baboons establish their social attachments and cohesiveness. However, grooming derives its significance from the presence of misery-inflicting parasites—fleas and ticks!

Perhaps we need the struggles that suffering brings. We are now entering into difficult economic and social times. If the comfort we extend to one another produces oneness, then the approaching trials will give us many opportunities. But first, we need the fleas and ticks to awaken our need for grooming!

Once, I read a fascinating article about a man watching a butterfly struggling to emerge from its cocoon:

> It seemed to take forever. Finally, being impatient and wanting to free the struggling insect, he took a knife and split the cocoon. The butterfly was born, but it could not fly. The man had prevented a very necessary struggle that the butterfly needed. The struggle forces body juices into the insect's wings, giving it the strength to fly.[1]

Perhaps suffering is a necessary gift while we are plagued in this life with the corruption that comes from sin and selfishness. Consider a world where there were no consequences for evil, where our conscience was never troubled, and where we would live forever without any infirmities. Sometimes, as I look upon my wife as she sleeps, I become aware once again that I will not always have her. This thought reminds me to cherish her before death takes one of us away.

Once sin had laid claim to Adam and Eve, God blocked them from the Garden of Eden and the tree-of-life so that they would not eat from the tree and live forever. Yes, death was a part of the curse, and it seems to have been a completely necessary component. The Apostle Paul explained the need for the Fall and death in Romans 8:

> Against its will, all creation was subjected to God's curse [the Fall]. But with eager hope, the creation looks forward to the day when it will join God's children in glorious freedom from death and decay. For we know that all creation has been groaning as in the pains of childbirth right up to the present time. And we believers also groan, even though we have the Holy Spirit within us as a foretaste of future glory, for we long for our bodies to be released from sin and suffering. We, too, wait with eager hope for the day when God will give us our full rights as his adopted children, including the new bodies he has promised us.
>
> ROMANS 8:20–23 NLT

Yes, suffering was the consequence of human sin. But it is that same suffering that impels us to long for deliverance. It resets our priorities on the things that really matter. Therefore, as we walk with God, we find ourselves hungering and thirsting for the promised glorious and eternal marriage to our Savior:

> Dear friends, don't be surprised at the fiery trials you are going through, as if something strange were happening to you. Instead, be very glad—for these trials make you partners with Christ in his suffering, so that you will have the wonderful joy of seeing his glory when it is revealed to all the world.
>
> 1 PETER 4:12–13 NLT

It will be a joy for us to finally receive what we have longed for. How is it that suffering can accomplish this and help us to endure the challenges of life so that we may receive our reward? Through suffering, the hope we have in ourselves is transferred to the hope we have in our Savior alone. We were created for love and devotion to God, and not for the self-sufficiency we normally crave.

Paul explained that suffering was necessary. Why? In order for him to learn that he couldn't trust in himself:

> We think you ought to know, dear brothers and sisters, about the trouble we went through in the province of Asia. We were crushed and overwhelmed beyond our ability to endure, and we thought we would never live through it. In fact, we expected to die. But as a result, we stopped relying on ourselves and learned to rely only on God, who raises the dead.
>
> 2 CORINTHIANS 1:8–9 NLT

Without suffering, we would never learn to trust God. It's just too convenient to trust in ourselves. I would like to believe that I have what it takes to successfully deal with all the challenges of life. However, such a trust in myself would prevent me from learning to cherish God and even others. Without suffering and the self-reflection that it brings, we would remain blind and proud. We would aggrandize ourselves, as kings often do:

> The people gave [King Herod] a great ovation, shouting, "It's the voice of a god, not of a man!" Instantly, an angel of the Lord struck Herod with a sickness, because he accepted the people's worship instead of giving the glory to God. So he was consumed with worms and died.
>
> ACTS 12:22–23 NLT

Herod's kingship had enabled him to think that he was a god, that he was free to diminish others and abuse them. This brings us to a common theme in the Bible. It seems inevitable that whenever Israel's stomach was full, they would forget about God. They would conclude that they had all that it takes to live a fulfilling life. Many of Jesus' parables indicate this:

Then Jesus told this story to some who had great confidence
in their own righteousness and scorned everyone else.

LUKE 18:9 NLT

Self-righteousness invariably involves the continual exercise of comparing
ourselves with others. We may begin to think that we require more of a
certain commodity than others, and when we have acquired it, we look
down on everyone else. However, Jesus concluded the previously-cited
parable like this:

"For those who exalt themselves will be humbled, and
those who humble themselves will be exalted."

MATTHEW 23:12 NIV

Humility is the soil from which every virtue must sprout. Humility is also a
matter of the truth. It provides us with the accurate self-knowledge of our
multiple inadequacies and moral failures. Through humility, we recognize
our utter dependence on God. Consequently, if we reject God, we are
also rejecting any valid self-knowledge, any knowledge of our true status.
When we reject God, it is impossible for us to recognize our inadequacies
and our utter need for Him. Without the love and reassurance of our
Savior, we flee from this painful knowledge and disdain humility.

~

Why then the need for suffering? We need suffering to shake us up. We
need suffering so that our eyes might be opened. For only then will we
invite God to do the work in us that will bring about change:

Before I was afflicted I went astray, but now I keep your
word. ... It is good for me that I was afflicted, so that I
might learn your statutes. The law of your mouth is better
to me than thousands of gold and silver pieces.

PSALM 119:67, 71–72 NASB

The Apostle Paul also taught that if we want to become more like Christ,
there is no way to bypass suffering:

[We are] always carrying in the body the death of Jesus, so
that the life of Jesus may also be manifested in our bodies.

> For we who live are always being given over to death for
> Jesus' sake, so that the life of Jesus also may be manifested
> in our mortal flesh.
>
> 2 CORINTHIANS 4:10–11

But how can we justify the great extent of such suffering? When we compare it with what we are promised in eternity, our suffering in this life no longer seems so great:

> Yet what we suffer now is nothing compared to the glory
> he will reveal to us later.
>
> ROMANS 8:18 NLT

Our hope rests in the bosom of eternity. It is the answer to all our pains. In comparison, our temporary suffering is a small price to pay for the harvest of eternal bliss.

We need a theology of suffering, and to understand it as a positive—not a negative—in the hands of our Savior. We need to regard our God as merciful and righteous, not any sort of cosmic kill-joy. He is training us for His Olympics, and this requires a lean diet.

ORIGINAL SIN

CHAPTER 2

Is "Original Sin" Unjust?

This charge against God's righteousness and justice seems insurmountable. The issue of "original sin" involves several distinct questions. Are we born ...

1.   ... subject to death?
2.   ... guilty of Adam's sin?
3.   ... under the condemnation of God?
4.   ... without the ability to choose God?
5.   ... with a sin nature?

Christians all accept the reality of the Fall and the resulting curses, including death. Yet, there are widely different understandings of the nature of "original sin." Consequently, numbers 2-5 of the questions in this list remain debatable. While many Protestants and the Catholic Church accept all five of the above, the Orthodox Church—and Judaism—rejects the last four:

> Adam and Eve committed a sin, the original sin. The Eastern Orthodox Church teaches that no one is guilty for the actual sin they committed but rather everyone inherits the consequences of this act; the foremost of this is physical death in this world. This is the reason why the original fathers of the Church over the centuries have preferred the term ancestral sin ... Since every human is a descendant of Adam then 'no one is free from the implications of this sin' (which is human death) ... While mortality is certainly a result of the Fall, along with this also what is termed

"concupiscence" in the writings of St Augustine of Hippo—
this is the "evil impulse" of Judaism, and in Orthodoxy, we
might say this is our "disordered passion." It isn't only that
we are born in death, or in a state of distance from God,
but also that we are born with disordered passion within
us. Orthodoxy would not describe the human state as one
of "total depravity."[1]

According to Orthodoxy, we weren't born guilty of Adam's sin, but we
have all received the penalty for his sin—death and "disordered passion."
So, even though these questions divide Bible-believing Christians, we
cannot ignore them. Too much is at stake:

- Some beliefs about original sin seem to compromise God's
  righteousness. They make it seem as if He has condemned the
  entire human race, even though we were born—according to
  some—with no choice but to reject Him.

- Numbers 2-5 seem to undermine the Bible's teaching about
  the extent of our guilt and our culpability. After all, if we were
  born as sinners with no chance of coming to God, then our
  culpability would be minimized—while God's culpability would
  be maximized.

One atheist summed up the problem like this:

> We are "guilty" of original sin just by being born
> human...someone can be guilty only of choosing to
> commit a particular criminal act. No one chooses to be
> born a human, with an allegedly corrupt, incorrigible
> "nature." Therefore original sin cannot be something we're
> "guilty" of and "deserve" punishment for.[2]

This understanding means that God has unjustly damned humanity,
which never even had a chance to come to Him to receive His mercy.

If we fail to address this doubt and the shadow it casts on God's
righteousness, it will continue to fester and invade the core of our faith.
Our confidence in God will most assuredly be shaken, and we will feel like
hypocrites when we tell others that God loves them. Therefore, we must
seek a solution.

Does the Bible explicitly teach the last four tenets, or questions?

Does the account of Adam's sin and the resulting Fall of humanity provide evidence for the last four items in the list? When we examine Genesis 3, we do not find any explicit proof that we were all born guilty of Adam's sin. Instead, we discover the advent of sin and death, the curse upon creation—including increased pain in childbearing—and banishment from the perfectly nurturing Garden of Eden and the presence of God.

Perhaps we do not need to have a sin nature to explain the fact that we sin. Adam and Eve did not need a "sin nature" to sin. Rather, they willingly sinned. They succumbed to their own temptation.

What do we mean by a "sin nature"? Even though Cain sinned, it doesn't seem that his nature had *compelled* him to sin. Even though it was after the Fall, God had informed Cain—plainly—that he alone was accountable for his sins. And the reason for his accountability? He had not followed God's directions. Cain had made an incorrect offering, unlike Abel. Therefore, God had rhetorically asked Cain:

> "Why are you angry, and why has your face fallen? If you do well, will you not be accepted? And if you do not do well, sin is crouching at the door. Its desire is contrary to you, but you must rule over it."
>
> GENESIS 4:6–7

According to God, Cain—a child of the Fall—was fully responsible for his behavior. As a result, he *never* responded to God like this: "God, you really can't blame me for what I did. It was *you* who imposed upon me a sin nature. *You* deprived me of any freewill to do good."

James makes it very clear in his warning—we should *not* make any excuses for our sins:

> Let no one say when he is tempted, "I am being tempted by God," for God cannot be tempted with evil, and he himself tempts no one. But each person is tempted when he is lured and enticed by his *own* desire. Then desire when it has conceived gives birth to sin, and sin when it is fully grown brings forth death.
>
> JAMES 1:13–15, *italics mine*

23

God did not insert evil desires into our DNA. Although humanity is depraved, it seems that this is not the result of being born with evil. Instead, we must take responsibility for our sinful desires and flee from them. Nor were we born dead in sin, unable and powerless to do otherwise! Instead, James claimed that death only occurs when our own desire gives birth to sin.

Therefore, we should never rationalize our sin, thinking, "It was Adam's bad choice and my own upbringing that made me do it." Instead, we must confess that our guilt is fully our own, just as David did in Psalms 32 and 51.

~

Is it possible that we are born incapable, not only of choosing God, but even of doing what is right? It seems that Scripture makes no allowance for this excuse:

> For the wrath of God is revealed from heaven against all ungodliness and unrighteousness of men, who by their unrighteousness suppress the truth. For what can be known about God is plain to them, because God has shown it to them. For his invisible attributes, namely, his eternal power and divine nature, have been clearly perceived, ever since the creation of the world, in the things that have been made. *So they are without excuse.*
>
> ROMANS 1:18–20, *italics mine*

Thus, the truth for us is plain to see—we are without any excuse for rejecting God. Consequently, we cannot disown our guilt for rejecting Him. We simply cannot say: "I was born with a sin nature. Therefore, it is not possible for me to choose God." If this were the case, then we would have a perfect excuse for our sins.

Israel had many excuses for their multiple wrong-doings, but they never resorted to this line of reasoning. It was not even on their radar. Why not? It must have been absolutely unthinkable to them. They understood that this kind of perspective had nothing to do with the revelation they had received from God. Instead, when Israel wandered into sin, there was no excuse they could fall back on. God had always laid the complete blame on them.

Superficially, it might seem to some that Israel did indeed have a Scriptural excuse for their sins. After all, hadn't God hardened their hearts? Here is what He had instructed Isaiah to preach to Israel:

> "Keep on hearing, but do not understand; keep on seeing, but do not perceive. Make the heart of this people dull, and their ears heavy, and blind their eyes; lest they see with their eyes, and hear with their ears, and understand with their hearts, and turn and be healed."
>
> ISAIAH 6:9–10

However, this wasn't God's verdict upon an innocent people. Instead, He was merely giving them over to the desire of their hearts, hearts which had already been hardened *by their own choices:*

> Therefore God gave them up in the lusts of their hearts to impurity, to the dishonoring of their bodies among themselves … For this reason God gave them up to dishonorable passions. For their women exchanged natural relations for those that are contrary to nature; and the men likewise gave up natural relations with women … And since they did not see fit to acknowledge God, God gave them up to a debased mind to do what ought not to be done.
>
> ROMANS 1:24–28
> *see also Psalm 69:22–23*

Thus, they would reap the very things they had sown. There is no indication that they had been born with hard hearts.

Besides all this, even ignorance of the law provided no excuse for Israel's sins, according to Romans 1:32 and 2:14-16. After an Israelite had become aware that he had sinned unknowingly, there was no way that he was absolved for his error. He was still required to sacrifice an animal and make reparations.

In addition, God had often claimed that He had given Israel everything they needed for their blessing:

"Let me sing for my beloved my love song concerning his vineyard: My beloved had a vineyard on a very fertile hill. He dug it and cleared it of stones, and planted it with choice vines; he built a watchtower in the midst of it, and hewed out a wine vat in it; and he looked for it to yield grapes, but it yielded wild grapes. And now, O inhabitants of Jerusalem and men of Judah, judge between me and my vineyard. What more was there to do for my vineyard, that I have not done in it? When I looked for it to yield grapes, why did it yield wild grapes?"

ISAIAH 5:1–4

God claimed that there was *nothing more He could have done* for Israel. There is no evidence that God had deprived His people of the ability to come to Him. Instead, they had been blinded by the hardness of their own unrepentant hearts. As a consequence, God laid the entire blame for their sins on His people, Israel:

"Yet I planted you [Israel] a choice vine, wholly of pure seed. How then have you turned degenerate and become a wild vine?"

JEREMIAH 2:21

The Israelites had not been born degenerate—*they became degenerate!* In a song that God had given Moses to teach His people and to testify against them, He blamed Israel for their degeneracy:

"The Rock, his work is perfect, for all his ways are justice. A God of faithfulness and without iniquity, just and upright is he. They have dealt corruptly with him; they [Israel] are no longer his children because they are blemished; they are a crooked and twisted generation."

DEUTERONOMY 32:4–5

Where did the prophets of Israel stand in all of this? The prophets never softened their indictment of Israel's unfaithfulness by saying, "I know you tried your best and were not able to do better. You were just born that way." Solomon also confirmed this verdict:

> See, this alone I found, that God made man upright, but
> they have sought out many schemes.
>
> ECCLESIASTES 7:29

According to the consistent message of the Scriptures, each one of us is at fault—not God. We deserve His condemnation:

> *Therefore you have no excuse,* O man, every one of you who
> judges. For in passing judgment on another you condemn
> yourself, because you, the judge, practice the very same
> things. *We know that the judgment of God rightly falls on*
> *those who practice such things.*
>
> ROMANS 2:1–2, *italics mine*

I am convinced that spiritual maturity requires us to take full responsibility for our sins. There is no way that we should be making any excuses for the wrongs we commit. Statements like the following are unacceptable and carry no weight before our holy God: "I was born into sin and couldn't have done otherwise."

◈

Lastly, we are without excuse because Jesus brought light into the world and confirmed it through His miracles:

> "If I had not come and spoken to them, they would not
> have been guilty of sin, but now they have no excuse for
> their sin. Whoever hates me hates my Father also. If I had
> not done among them the works that no one else did, they
> would not be guilty of sin, but now they have seen and
> hated both me and my Father. But the word that is written
> in their Law must be fulfilled: 'They hated me *without*
> *a cause.*'"
>
> JOHN 15:22–25, *italics mine*

Israel had not been born with an inherent hatred of God. According to Romans, it seems that we were born "alive"—free from His wrath—not spiritually dead:

> And I was *alive* apart from the law once: but when the
> commandment came, sin revived, and I died; and the
> commandment, which was unto life, this I found to
> be unto death: for sin, finding occasion, through the
> commandment beguiled me, and through it *slew me.*
>
> ROMANS 7:9–11 ASV, *italics mine*
> see also Romans 6:16

Paul, speaking for all humanity, claimed that he had been spiritually
"alive" when he was born. There is no indication that he had been born
under God's wrath. It was only later that sin did, in a spiritual sense, slay
him. Likewise:

> They are darkened in their understanding, alienated from
> the life of God because of the ignorance that is in them,
> due to their hardness of heart. *They have become callous*
> and have given themselves up to sensuality, greedy to
> practice every kind of impurity.
>
> EPHESIANS 4:18–19, *italics mine*

Notice that we were "darkened," not because we were born that way, but
because of "the ignorance that is in them due to their hardness of heart."
Once again, were we born with this hardness? No! Scripture says it best:
"They have become callous and have given themselves up to sensuality ... "

God did not bring us into the world in a "darkened" or hard-hearted
condition. There is no indication of that. Instead, our hearts have "become
calloused."

Three Problem Verses

PSALM 51:5

*Behold, I was brought forth in iniquity, and in sin did my mother
conceive me.*

It is impossible to understand this verse literally; that is, in the sense that
David was blaming his mother. The entire Psalm rejects the idea that
David had been blame-shifting to his mother, or that he was mitigating
his guilt by claiming that he had been born with a sinful nature. Instead,

it should be understood hyperbolically. David is merely confessing that he had been sinning from his earliest years.

EPHESIANS 2:3

> ... among whom we all once lived in the passions of our flesh, carrying out the desires of the body and the mind, and were by nature children of wrath, like the rest of mankind.

This verse does not say that we were *born* "by nature children of wrath." In keeping with the context, we had *become* "children of wrath."

ROMANS 5:18–19

> Therefore, as one trespass led to condemnation for all men, so one act of righteousness leads to justification and life for all men. For as by the one man's disobedience the many were made sinners, so by the one man's obedience the many will be made righteous.
>
> See also 1 Corinthians 15:22.

These verses are not explicit about how Adam's sin led to the condemnation of the rest of humanity. But the parallel that Paul draws between Adam and Jesus is very helpful. It seems best to understand that, as life in Jesus requires an intermediary step of faith, so too would death through Adam also require an *intermediate* step—our own sins:

JESUS' ATONEMENT → THROUGH FAITH → BRINGS JUSTIFICATION

ADAM'S SIN → THROUGH OUR OWN SIN → BRINGS CONDEMNATION

Paul seems to endorse this parallel between Adam and Jesus:

> Therefore, just as sin came into the world through one man, and death through sin, and so death spread to all men because *all sinned* ...
>
> ROMANS 5:12, *italics mine*

Perhaps death would also come to us because we willingly endorsed Adam's sin. If this is so, then how would we do that? By committing our own sins and thereby confirming God's just verdict, resulting in the Fall and death. Besides, humanity's intimate relationship with God had been disrupted through the Fall and the expulsion from Eden, making our own fall into sin almost inevitable. Thus, we died through Adam! Nevertheless, God graciously provided men and women the means by which they could confess and turn from their sins.

~

Admittedly, my treatment of Romans 5 will not persuade all. However, the preponderance of evidence from the Bible *completely exonerates God*. At the same time, that same evidence rightly accuses us of rebellion against Him. In the final analysis, He alone is entirely righteous:

> This is the message we have heard from him and proclaim
> to you, that God is light, and in him is no darkness at all.
>
> 1 JOHN 1:5

I prefer this understanding because it doesn't impugn God's righteousness. The entire blame is placed on us, exactly where it belongs. And what's more, that blame is entirely corroborated by Scripture. In conclusion, there is no injustice in God, but in us!

The skeptic is thus deprived of any excuse. He simply cannot say: "God has no right to judge me for rejecting Him. He stacked the deck against me." Paul implies that if God had been unjust, He would have disqualified Himself from judging the world:

> But if our unrighteousness serves to show the righteousness
> of God, what shall we say? That God is unrighteous
> to inflict wrath on us? (I speak in a human way.) By no
> means! For then how could God judge the world [if He
> is unrighteous]?
>
> ROMANS 3:5–6
> *see also Genesis 18:25 and Deuteronomy 32:4*

Bringing us into the world without any capacity to choose God and then condemning us for not doing what we couldn't possibly do does not comport with any understanding of justice. Nor does such an idea agree with biblical revelation. Instead, the entire Bible requires us to take full responsibility for our sins. We have absolutely no grounds upon which we may blame God, the Fall, the devil, our parents, or anyone else.

SALVATION

CHAPTER 3

Is the Doctrine of Election Unjust?

Different terms are used to refer to this doctrine: predestination, eternal security, and election. It seems that God must choose us—since it is apparent that we do not choose Him:

> ...as it is written: "None is righteous, no, not one; no one understands; no one seeks for God. All have turned aside; together they have become worthless; no one does good, not even one." "Their throat is an open grave; they use their tongues to deceive." "The venom of asps is under their lips." "Their mouth is full of curses and bitterness." "Their feet are swift to shed blood; in their paths are ruin and misery, and the way of peace they have not known." "There is no fear of God before their eyes."
>
> ROMANS 3:10–18

> The natural person [lacking the Spirit] does not accept the things of the Spirit of God, for they are folly to him, and he is not able to understand them because they are spiritually discerned.
>
> 1 CORINTHIANS 2:14

Many regard this doctrine, as well as the God Who implemented it, as unjust. The following is typical of the many responses from skeptics I have seen down through the years:

> *This means that, if I am not among the predestined, I have no chance at all at salvation. Therefore, I am punished because God didn't choose me. This is the height of injustice, and your God of love is a hypocrite!*

35

Who is to be blamed for our condemnation—God or us? Even though we will all reject God—a point that I will try to make in this chapter—does the fault lie with the Creator, or with His creation? Shouldn't the Designer be held accountable if all the people He has designed reject Him? This question will be addressed at the end of the chapter.

Here is a simplified chronological "timetable" for the way this works out, according to the Bible:

1. Free to choose, all reject God and thus deserve His wrath.
2. God has mercy on some and regenerates their hearts so that they will believe what they had rejected.

First of all, there is nothing illogical, unjust, or hypocritical about this. Item #1 pertains to justice, and God doesn't need to grade on a curve. Instead:

> For the wages of sin is death, but the free gift of God is eternal life in Christ Jesus our Lord.
>
> ROMANS 6:23

Even one sin warrants death before an all-righteous and just God (*see James 2:10*).

Furthermore, #2 is not about justice but grace, and isn't grace free to discriminate among all those who need mercy?

> What shall we say then? Is there injustice on God's part? By no means! For he says to Moses, "I will have mercy on whom I have mercy, and I will have compassion on whom I have compassion." So then it depends not on human will or exertion, but on God, who has mercy.
>
> ROMANS 9:14–16

Unlike justice, *mercy—a correlative of grace—can discriminate*. It is like giving a party and inviting your closest friends. You do not need to be just for such an occasion. There is no need for you to treat everyone by the same standard and thus invite the entire city. No one could fault you for not doing so. This also means that God is free to invite to His everlasting banquet anyone He wishes—among those who had initially rejected Him.

This also means that we have no basis for charging God with injustice for not predestining us all to salvation. Once again, this is a matter of grace, not justice. If God were only just, He would have destroyed the entire human race. Therefore, the skeptics among us must realize that we had already been given a chance to come to God in faith. Instead, we rebelled against the Truth (*see Romans 1:18–32*).

This is shocking to us. Is humanity really that bad that God would place us all under condemnation? Before we answer this question, we must be reminded of a simple truth: we do not see the inner man. We—even the most spiritual among us—are duped by appearances. The prophet Samuel certainly was! God had to warn him against any sort of judgment according to "outward appearance" (*see 1 Samuel 16:7*).

Perhaps all of us judge superficially, and therefore cannot fully appreciate the depths of our sin and God's abhorrence of it. Jeremiah had a hard time accepting God's dismal evaluation of Israel. God therefore challenged him:

> "Go up and down the streets of Jerusalem, look around and consider, search through her squares. If you can find but one person who deals honestly and seeks the truth, I will forgive this city."
>
> JEREMIAH 5:1

Jeremiah's appraisal of humanity was far too high, especially concerning his own people. He thought it would be easy to find one honest man:

> I thought, "These are only the poor; they are foolish, for they do not know the way of the Lord, the requirements of their God. So I will go to the leaders and speak to them; surely they know the way of the Lord, the requirements of their God."
>
> JEREMIAH 5:4–5

Because of Jeremiah's inflated assessment of educated Israelites, he found God's appraisal and judgment unbelievable and unduly harsh. However, Jeremiah discovered that all of Israel was in rebellion against the Lord. Furthermore, Jeremiah found out that even his own family wanted to kill him for proclaiming God's message.

However, once Jeremiah began to see the extent of human rebellion, he reassessed his view of humanity and began to affirm God's righteous judgments. In fact, he began to plead with God *not to forgive*:

> LORD, you know all about their murderous plots against me. Don't forgive their crimes and blot out their sins. Let them die before you. Deal with them in your anger.
>
> JEREMIAH 18:23 NLT

∽

If we could only see the full extent of human rebellion and our hatred of the Savior, perhaps we might regard predestination as Good News, which it truly is. Perhaps we might come to appreciate the extreme generosity of God's mercy.

It is imperative that we understand the depths of our hatred of the light and our enmity against God, no matter how offensive this exercise might be. When we come to understand the extent of God's forgiveness of our sins in light of this, then we will be truly grateful. If we fail to perceive this, then our tendency will be to vastly undervalue God's grace.

Jesus was invited to a top-of-the-line Pharisaic lunch. A woman He had evidently previously forgiven entered, uninvited. She proceeded to anoint His feet with expensive oil. The host was appalled because Jesus had allowed such a base creature to touch Him. Jesus responded by explaining that the woman was more blessed than the host:

> "He who is forgiven little, loves little."
>
> LUKE 7:47

The woman loved much because she knew that she had been forgiven much. Often, we do not realize the extent to which we have sinned and then have been forgiven. Therefore, we love little and disdain God's just ways. If we only understood the full measure of Christ's forgiveness, we would not be offended by God's judgments. We would know that His judgments are just. We would fully accept the Bible's judgment in Romans 6:23 and Deuteronomy 27:26 that sin deserves death. We would also gladly embrace whatever mercy that God might offer—even predestination.

There is also another danger that occurs when we fail to appreciate the extent of our rebellion against the light—boasting! For my first 15 years in Christ, I believed that I had chosen Christ and not the other way around. And why had I chosen Christ? I had convinced myself that it was because I was more spiritual than others. In doing this, I exalted myself and, like the tax collector in Luke 18:9-14, I looked down on others. As a consequence, I had to suffer for years before I could recognize that I had been boasting. Furthermore, this boasting was offensive to the One who had given me the faith to believe in the first place.

The same had been true for King Nebuchadnezzar, the great Babylonian empire-builder. Understandably, he was convinced that he was great, and that his greatness was all about him. However, he had a disturbing dream which changed everything. Daniel interpreted it for him:

> It is a decree of the Most High, which has come upon my lord the king, that you shall be driven from among men, and your dwelling shall be with the beasts of the field. You shall be made to eat grass like an ox, and you shall be wet with the dew of heaven, and seven periods of time shall pass over you, till you know that the Most High rules the kingdom of men and gives it to whom he will.
>
> DANIEL 4:24–25

For seven years, Nebuchadnezzar lost his mind, thinking that he was a cow. Why had God punished him in this manner? Because of his belligerent behavior? Because he took Israel into captivity? Was it his treatment of the poor? No! It happened so that he could learn a theological lesson: any success he had wasn't about Him but about God, who chooses "whom He will"!

At the end of the seven years of grievous suffering, Nebuchadnezzar's sanity returned. He learned the lesson and gave all of the thanks to God for choosing him. If this pagan, unenlightened by Scripture, was held to account for his boasting, then we will—even more so—be held accountable.

Why? Because God deserves all the credit! What if someone were to give you a magnificent painting from their studio, and you hang it up in your house. When friends come for a visit and ask you about the masterpiece, should you take the credit for painting it? If you do, wouldn't the real artist be offended? Likewise, if faith is God's gift to us, as these verses proclaim—Ephesians 2:8-9; Philippians 1:29; Acts 13:48; 16:14; 18:27—and if we take credit for it, as I had, would God not have every right to be offended?

It is only fitting that we give God all the credit for our salvation, and even for the faith to receive it—God's predestined salvation!

Is predestination biblical?

Here are a few verses that claim that it is completely biblical. None seek after God (Romans 3:10-18). Therefore, election cannot be a matter of God choosing us based upon His foreknowledge that we would choose Him. Why not? Simply this: we would never choose Him!

> But God chose what is foolish in the world to shame the wise; God chose what is weak in the world to shame the strong; God chose what is low and despised in the world, even things that are not, to bring to nothing things that are, so that no human being might boast in the presence of God.
>
> 1 CORINTHIANS 1:27–29

God purposely elected those who are the least deserving, at least by human standards. Why did He do this? To make it harder for the chosen to arrogantly boast, "God chose me because I deserve it."

I used to believe that God chose me because I was more spiritual than others. However, in retrospect, I now understand that He had to break me down and humble me before He could rebuild me (Luke 18:14). He showed me in the most painful ways how undeserving I really am. Had He not performed His spiritual surgery on me, any good thing would have gone to my foolish head to convince me of my spiritual superiority.

God is intent on depriving us of any basis for boasting. Before Jacob and Esau had been born and had done anything worthy of merit, He revealed to their mother Rebecca that Jacob would be the child of the Promise:

> When Rebekah had conceived children by one man, our forefather Isaac, though they were not yet born and had done nothing either good or bad—in order that God's

purpose of election might continue, not because of works but because of him who calls—she was told, "The older [Esau] will serve the younger [Jacob]."

ROMANS 9:10–12

God chose Jacob over the firstborn Esau to establish that His choice had nothing to do with performance or merit. Nor can His election be based upon something good that God foresees in us. If this were the case, then we would have a reason to boast; and election would not be about His sovereign grace but our future merit. Scripture is clear on this:

> ... [It was God] who saved us and called us to a holy calling, not because of our works but because of his own purpose and grace, which he gave us in Christ Jesus before the ages began.

2 TIMOTHY 1:9

> ... even as he chose us in him before the foundation of the world, that we should be holy and blameless before him. In love he predestined us for love and adoption as sons through Jesus Christ, according to the purpose of his will.

EPHESIANS 1:4–5

The choice is His and not ours, as Jesus proclaimed:

> "You did not choose me, but I chose you and appointed you that you should go and bear fruit and that your fruit should abide, so that whatever you ask the Father in my name, he may give it to you."

JOHN 15:16

Even faith does not start with us and our choice of God, but with God:

> But to all who did receive him, who believed in his name, he gave the right to become children of God, who were born, not of blood nor of the will of the flesh nor of the will of man, but of God.

JOHN 1:12–13

But don't we at least have to supply the faith? Fundamentally, even our faith comes as a gift from God:

41

> For by grace you have been saved through faith. And this is not your own doing; it is the gift of God, not a result of works, so that no one may boast.
>
> EPHESIANS 2:8–9

Shouldn't the Designer be held accountable if all reject Him?

Should God be accountable if all sin, especially since the first couple sinned and death and derangement was passed on to all? Couldn't God's original design have been better? Doesn't He deserve at least some blame for the fact that all had initially—even freely—rejected Him? I don't think that we have the wisdom to evaluate His possible designs. It is enough to note that any object, as useful and perfectly designed as it might be, can be misused to cause harm. This is certainly true of our freewill, which has been used to cause great suffering and harm.

Still, could God have chosen a better alternative? Why did God not create humanity like He created the obedient angels in heaven? Perhaps God had good reasons for not making us that way. Perhaps the ultimate good He had planned could not have been realized without an initial descent into sin and corruption. To bake bread requires kneading the dough and getting our hands dirty with flour. Perhaps an enduring joy, love, and peace also requires us to first get our hands dirty. Perhaps we first had to be humbled to prepare us for our glorious eternity:

> "Whoever exalts himself will be humbled, and whoever humbles himself will be exalted."
>
> MATTHEW 23:12

Clearly, there is a lot we do not understand. To think that we have a firm grasp on these issues can get us into a lot of trouble. Arrogance regarding our understanding has often backfired. It did exactly that with the most righteous man on all the earth, Job. He was convinced that his suffering was God's fault. He even accused Him of injustice.

Finally, Job got what he asked for—a private audience with God. However, when God finally arrived, He rebuked Job for speaking so foolishly:

> Then the LORD answered Job out of the whirlwind
> and said: "Who is this that darkens counsel by words
> without knowledge?"
>
> JOB 38:1–2

God then asked Job a series of about 60 questions, none of which Job could answer. Job got the point and repented for the hubris he had displayed by judging God.

Are we demanding too much understanding of God, even more than we demand of science? I think so. There is a lot we can learn, but to demand *a complete answer from God* is to proceed beyond reason. We need to recognize and appreciate our humble status. Nevertheless, He encourages us to seek wisdom and understanding:

> ... yes, if you call out for insight
> and raise your voice for understanding,
> if you seek it like silver
> and search for it as for hidden treasures,
> then you will understand the fear of the LORD
> and find the knowledge of God.
> For the LORD gives wisdom;
> from his mouth come knowledge and understanding ...
>
> PROVERBS 2:3–6

CHAPTER 4

Does God's Foreknowledge Detract from Our Freewill?

An important element of any defense of God—and the Bible, as well—is our freewill. Because we have freewill and freely choose to sin, we are the guilty party! No blame is to be placed on the Creator, who made everything "very good" (Genesis 1:31). Besides, if evil is the fault of God, then God is not entirely righteous.

Every biblical commandment is predicated on the assumption that our freewill choices matter. This is why we are justly culpable for making the wrong choice:

> "… choose this day whom you will serve, whether the gods your fathers served in the region beyond the River, or the gods of the Amorites in whose land you dwell. But as for me and my house, we will serve the LORD."
>
> JOSHUA 24:15

God invariably treats us as if we have freewill. However, if God has perfect foreknowledge—omniscience—then each of us will do exactly as He knows we will do. Doesn't this mean that we lack the freewill to do otherwise? And, if that is the case, then wouldn't God's foreknowledge implicate Him in our wrongdoing?

Not at all! Even though we will do exactly what God knows we will do, *this does not mean that we couldn't have done otherwise* at the time. *It's just that we wouldn't have done otherwise,* even though we end up doing exactly what God knew we would do.

For example, my wife knows that when I go out to buy milk, I will wear something on my feet to protect them from the snow. While I *could* have gone out to buy the milk barefooted—I had the freewill to do this—she knows for certain that I *wouldn't* have done so. Therefore, her foreknowledge of my behavior does not detract from my freewill. Instead, they can co-exist.

Even if God knows with greater certainty—and He does because He is not limited by time since He created it—God's foreknowledge does not detract from my freewill. Similarly, my wife knows that I *wouldn't* go barefoot in the snow! *Knowing* the outcome is not the same as *causing* the outcome. It simply represents God's foreknowledge of how I will exercise my freewill.

The intuition that we have freewill is so basic, to doubt it would require that we doubt every other basic thing that we know about ourselves. Things like the following would cease to be certainties:

- *I am a distinct person.*
- *I can trust my memory in most instances.*
- *I can trust my sight and my other senses.*

To doubt these things would also bring doubt upon every decision we make. We would even be compelled to doubt the very concept of doubt itself! Such a stultifying mind-set would make any life unlivable.

CHAPTER 5

Is the Requirement
of Faith for Salvation Unjust?

The God of the Bible has made faith a necessary element of salvation:

> "For God so loved the world, that he gave his only Son, that *whoever believes in him* should not perish but have eternal life."
>
> JOHN 3:16, *italics mine*

> For *by grace you have been saved through faith.* And this is not your own doing; it is the gift of God, not a result of works, so that no one may boast.
>
> EPHESIANS 2:8–9, *italics mine*

Many regard the requirement of faith as superficial, unnecessary, irrelevant, and even unjust. They claim that it is more important to live virtuously than to believe correctly. Consequently, there are some who demean faith and belief as merely a form of head-knowledge. Even worse, these same people are of the opinion that it is wrong to require everyone to believe what they find to be unbelievable. And finally, there are those who are convinced that to be punished for not believing is absolutely unfair. Instead, they feel that the emphasis should be on acts of love. For example, Oprah Winfrey has claimed that beliefs are not important, especially compared to a loving heart:

> "God is about a feeling experience, *not a believing experience.* ... A mistake we humans make is believing that there is only one way ... There are many paths to what you

47

call God ... *There couldn't possibly be just one way ...* Do you think that if you never heard the name of Jesus but lived with a loving heart ... you wouldn't get to heaven? ... *Does God care about the heart or if you call His Son 'Jesus?'*"[1] *(emphasis mine)*

Is God unjust for making faith, or belief, a requirement?

Concerning those who cannot believe what they regard as unbelievable—why should they be condemned? Is this fair? Yes. According to the Scriptures, there is an abundance of evidence that God exists. The following verse is but one example of many that prove this point:

> The heavens declare the glory of God, and the sky above proclaims his handiwork.
>
> PSALM 19:1

Therefore, when we disbelieve, we do so willingly, despite the evidence. But why would we do this? It's simple—we do it because we want to:

> For the wrath of God is revealed from heaven against all ungodliness and unrighteousness of men, who by their unrighteousness suppress the truth. For what can be known about God is plain to them, because God has shown it to them. For his invisible attributes, namely, his eternal power and divine nature, have been clearly perceived, ever since the creation of the world, in the things that have been made. So they are without excuse.
>
> ROMANS 1:18–20

Therefore, a lack of faith is a matter of *refusing to have faith,* and disregarding the many evidences.

We are surrounded by the evidence for God. Everything seems to have been designed, from the smallest atom to the fine-tuning of the universe and the elegant laws of science. In fact, there is no evidence for anything that is undesigned. We are engulfed by the knowledge of God, but we reject and suppress it. We are even aware that He will judge us for our denial of the truth:

> Though they know God's righteous decree that those who
> practice such things deserve to die, they not only do them
> but give approval to those who practice them.
>
> ROMANS 1:32

No wonder that the God of the Bible is hated! No one wants to be judged
and condemned. However, the Bible insists that we have absolutely no
rational or evidential grounds for disbelief. Speaking with the Athenian
philosophers on Mars Hill, the Apostle Paul made his case for the biblical
God based upon what they already knew about the nature of God:

> " ... for 'In him we live and move and have our being'; as
> even some of your own poets have said, "'For we are indeed
> his offspring.' Being then God's offspring, we ought not to
> think that the divine being is like gold or silver or stone, an
> image formed by the art and imagination of man. The times
> of ignorance God overlooked, but now he commands all
> people everywhere to repent, because he has fixed a day on
> which he will judge the world in righteousness by a man
> whom he has appointed; and of this he has given assurance
> to all by raising him from the dead."
>
> ACTS 17:28–31

If we are the "offspring" of the Creator, then how could we ever think that
it was wooden idols or mindless energy forces that created us? First of all,
the "cause" is always greater than the "effect." This is consistent with our
observations of the world and the findings of all the sciences. If the effect is
greater than the cause, then some aspect of the effect must be uncaused—a
possibility that science does not acknowledge.

Paul then appealed to the evidence—the resurrection of Jesus. Elsewhere,
the apostle had claimed that if anyone had any doubts about the
resurrection, there were many still alive—at that time—who could
corroborate this truth. After all, on just one occasion, there were some
five hundred people who had encountered Jesus after his resurrection,
according to 1 Corinthians 15:1-8. So much for the mass hypnosis theory!

Even from the depths of our being, we know that a righteous God exists,
but we prefer the darkness to the revealing light of God (John 3:19-20).
Many atheists openly acknowledge that they do not want God to exist. For

example, New York University Professor Emeritus of Philosophy, Thomas Nagel, asserted that no one can be impartial about God—at least the God of the Bible:

> I am talking of ... the fear of religion itself. I speak from experience, being strongly subject to this fear myself: I want atheism to be true ... It isn't just that I don't believe in God and, naturally hope there is no God! I don't want there to be a God. I don't want the universe to be like that ... I am curious whether there is anyone who is genuinely indifferent as to whether there is a God.[2]

Non-belief in our Creator is a refusal to believe and acknowledge our debt to Him. Therefore, a lack of faith in Him is simply one's refusal to have that faith.

Do we all need the mercy of God, or could we be good enough or loving enough to merit it, as Oprah claimed?

According to the entirety of Scriptural revelation, we all fall short of God's standards:

> ... as it is written: "None is righteous, no, not one; no one understands; no one seeks for God. All have turned aside; together they have become worthless; no one does good, not even one."
>
> ROMANS 3:10–12

> Enter not into judgment with your servant, for no one living is righteous before you.
>
> PSALM 130:3–4;
> *see also Psalm 143:2*

Jesus concluded one of His parables by claiming that we must regard ourselves as unworthy of God:

> "So you also, when you have done all that you were commanded, say, 'We are unworthy servants; we have only done what was our duty.'"
>
> LUKE 17:10

None of us are worthy of God or His salvation. Nevertheless, every religion of the world sets forth criteria by which humanity can climb their way up to the Divine through good deeds or other metrics. Despite the many ways that we have of assuring ourselves that we are deserving of God's approval, our conscience is continually crying out against this hubris:

> Even Gentiles, who do not have God's written law, show that they know his law when they instinctively obey it, even without having heard it. They demonstrate that God's law is written in their hearts, for their own conscience and thoughts either accuse them or tell them they are doing right.
>
> ROMANS 2:14–15 NLT

Even though our conscience condemns us, we refuse its message that we are unworthy of anything good from God (Romans 6:23; 3:23). Consequently, we are beset by guilt and shame, and we are desperate for approval. We try to cover over our moral inadequacies with the fig leaves of self-deception (Genesis 3). Therefore, many try to believe that they are good without even a shred of evidential support. They try, in vain, to find their worth within themselves. Thus, we condemn ourselves to an unnecessary and perpetual internal struggle for validation. Finally, we suppress anything that might contradict this false and inflated identity we have chosen for ourselves.

Instead of a strategy of self-aggrandizement, others find relief by denying freewill. They believe that they are compelled to act solely according to their instincts. One atheist admitted to me that this was how he was able to mitigate his feelings of failure, guilt, and shame.

Instead of these and other similar defensive maneuvers, our only hope is in the mercy of God through faith!

Our beliefs matter profoundly!

According to Oprah, our beliefs do not matter. It is our heart and loving deeds that are most important. However, our beliefs matter to God:

As we have already said, so now I say again: If anybody is preaching to you a gospel other than what you accepted, let him be eternally condemned!

GALATIANS 1:9

"I told you that you would die in your sins; if you do not believe that I am the one I claim to be, you will indeed die in your sins."

JOHN 8:24

Why do our beliefs matter to God? Before we can ever begin to recognize the answer to this question, we need to identify the problem that has alienated us from our only Hope:

If we say we have no sin, we deceive ourselves, and the truth is not in us. If we confess our sins, he is faithful and just to forgive us our sins and to cleanse us from all unrighteousness.

1 JOHN 1:8–9

Our beliefs are the lens through which we see and identify our problems— our alienation from ourselves and from God. Once we see the issues at hand, we can appropriately address them.

Beliefs also serve as a necessary foundation for love, virtue, and an accurate self-understanding. Our beliefs can chasten our pride and arrogance, which only serve to alienate others from us. Sometimes with great pain, our beliefs inform us that we are not worthy. In fact, we learn again and again that we have many of the same weaknesses for which we criticize others.

You might be thinking, "How depressing." But what if it is the truth? And what if this truth is essential for our virtue and for the thriving of our relationships? I have discovered that a low, yet accurate, self-estimation has served me well in many ways. First, it has enabled me to accept myself as I am. How? I have been assured that God loves me, despite my many flaws and failures. This has been so liberating for me. This self-acceptance has also helped me—a highly critical person—to accept the failings of others, including the shortcomings of my wife. It has also enabled me to examine and appraise myself honestly. This can be painful, but it has also blessed our marriage in many ways.

I no longer need to prove my worthiness, which had formerly been the motivation for all my good deeds. Therefore, my supposedly loving acts had not been other-centered but rather, self-centered. I thought I was being virtuous, but it was all a performance for my own benefit, that I might be enabled to live with myself. The recipient of my "virtuous deeds" was merely a vehicle through which I could build up my own ego.

But that was then; now I am free:

> So Jesus said to the Jews who had believed him, "If you abide in my word, you are truly my disciples, and you will know the truth, and the truth will set you free."
>
> JOHN 8:31–32

Here is just a small sampling of verses that I found to be liberating:

> "I have been crucified with Christ. It is no longer I who live, but Christ who lives in me. And the life I now live in the flesh I live by faith in the Son of God, who loved me and gave himself for me."
>
> GALATIANS 2:20

This verse enabled me to turn from my self-obsession to a healthy obsession with God—an utter delight!

> But he said to me, "My grace is sufficient for you, for my power is made perfect in weakness." Therefore I will boast all the more gladly of my weaknesses, so that the power of Christ may rest upon me. For the sake of Christ, then, I am content with weaknesses, insults, hardships, persecutions, and calamities. For when I am weak, then I am strong.
>
> 2 CORINTHIANS 12:9–10

Because God is more than enough for me, I no longer need to regard my weaknesses and insecurities as negative. Looked at in the right way, they can be viewed as positive.

> There is therefore now no condemnation for those who are
> in Christ Jesus.
>
> ROMANS 8:1

When I realized that the condemnation that I had been experiencing didn't come from God but from me, I felt liberated.

We cannot earn salvation. If we believe that we can, it will inevitably make us either boastful and arrogant, or depressed—once we realize how futile it is to try and earn it. Here is what the Word has to say:

> Then what becomes of our boasting? It is excluded. By
> what kind of law? By a law of works? No, but by the law of
> [the gift of] faith. For we hold that one is justified [saved]
> by faith apart from works of the law.
>
> ROMANS 3:27–28

Is this unjust? No! If God were to be just and give us what we deserve, He would destroy all of us as the sinners that we are (Romans 6:23). However, God is also merciful. His salvation and love are all about His undeserved mercy.

~

God's justice is severe, and justice must be administered equally to all. He is also entirely righteous. Therefore, according to Jesus, any one sin can damn us:

> But I say to you that everyone who is angry with his brother
> will be liable to judgment; whoever insults his brother will
> be liable to the council; and whoever says, 'You fool!' will
> be liable to the hell of fire.
>
> MATTHEW 5:22
> *see also James 2:10 and Deuteronomy 27:26*

You might not like this God. However, this is the God whom we must all face. Even though His standards are perfection, His mercy and forgiveness are without end:

"Go, and proclaim these words toward the north, and say, 'Return, faithless Israel,' declares the LORD. 'I will not look on you in anger, for I am merciful,' declares the LORD; 'I will not be angry forever. Only acknowledge your guilt, that you rebelled against the LORD your God and scattered your favors among foreigners under every green tree, and that you have not obeyed my voice,' declares the LORD.'"

JEREMIAH 3:12–13

Faith is a cause, but it is also the result of a greater cause—the regeneration of our inmost being to love, adore, and understand the One who gave His life for us. It is the cry of the blind: "Now I can see!"

CHAPTER 6

Could God Save, Apart from the Cross?

Why couldn't an omnipotent and loving God just forgive, apart from faith in Jesus' atonement? Tony Jones, an Emergent Church guru, questions the necessity of the death of Christ—substitutionary atonement—for the forgiveness of the sins of the world:

> I do not think that a bloody, violent death of a divine being was the only way to save the world. I believe that God has more freedom than that.[1]

Perhaps Jones has an incorrect understanding of "freedom." Biblically-speaking, while God can do anything He wants, He does not want to do everything. Some things would contradict His promises; others would contradict His character.

For one thing, God will not sin. This might seem like a limitation to His freedom. However, freedom loses all of its meaning if God is *totally* free to do anything. The game of chess loses all its meaning if we can move the pieces in any way we like, and whenever we like. In light of this, freedom only has meaning in the context of limitation.

Jesus understood this. He didn't want to go to the cross, and therefore He prayed:

> Going a little farther, he fell with his face to the ground and prayed, "My Father, if it is possible, may this cup be taken from me. Yet not as I will, but as you will."
>
> MATTHEW 26:39

Yet, there was no other way!

Why couldn't the omnipotent God have done it another way, as Jones suggests?

Evidently, it was necessary that Christ die for our sins. God's holy character required it:

> God presented Christ as a sacrifice of atonement, through the shedding of his blood—to be received by faith. He did this to demonstrate his righteousness, because in his forbearance he had left the sins committed beforehand unpunished—he did it to demonstrate his righteousness at the present time, so as to be just and the one who justifies those who have faith in Jesus.
>
> ROMANS 3:25-26

God must act justly! Do we understand this? Not really! There is no way that we can fully understand the character of God. Rather, those of us who know Him simply accept this! We accept our friends for who they are— why not also God?

God also required that Christ die for us to prove that He loves us.
—John 3:16 and Romans 5:8-10—

For me, this was no mere academic issue. It had been a matter of life and death. In deep pain and despair, I was unable to shake the thought that God might be a sadist, sitting on a cloud with a big bowl of popcorn, watching the freak show He had created for His entertainment. Perhaps the Bible was also a great deception, concocted by the master deceiver? After all, if God is all-powerful, then He would definitely have incredible powers of deception.

However, one night during prayer, He revealed something to me from His Word that made all the difference. He had died for me while I was still His enemy. Deceivers, con-artists, and sadists would never do such a thing. Besides, His death and suffering on the cross was the greatest conceivable price He could pay.

Something else became apparent to me. Had Jesus been a mere created being, it wouldn't have cost God anything to send Him to the cross, since He could have created 50,000 "saviors" in just a moment of time. Such a "sacrifice" would not have been any sort of demonstration of His love (Romans 5:7-10). Instead, the lamb for the sacrifice had to be God Himself.

This understanding freed me to believe in the love of Christ for undeserving people like me. Furthermore, I have never found anything else that would have convinced me that God truly loved me. Even His miraculous answers to my prayers might have been part of His deception. Apart from the Cross, I would never have been liberated from the doubt that my Savior might be a master deceiver, as the Muslims believe about Allah.

Is God unjust for not providing other ways to be eternally saved?

> Jesus said to him, "I am the way, and the truth, and the life. No one comes to the Father except through me."
>
> JOHN 14:6

Jesus is the one door through which we must pass to enter salvation. To logically answer the charge that this "exclusivity" is unjust, we would need to compare God's ways against an absolute moral law delineating what would be just. But do we have such a model or law? Is it possible to obtain a model more authoritative and perfect than what we have in the Bible? Today, we don't even believe that there is an absolute moral stricture against murder. Instead, even this issue has become a matter of pragmatics, of what works. In fact, it seems that society has already voted. By virtue of the 63 million murders of convenience through abortion in the Uniteed States, it seems that there are no absolute moral standards. All we have are ever-evolving laws.

How then can we bring our flimsy accusations against God?

CHAPTER 7

Is Universalism Biblical?

Universalism has become fantastically popular in the multicultural West. The following would be a fairly representative statement from someone who espoused that philosophy: "In the end, any God worth His salt wouldn't judge His children. A loving God would never condemn anyone to eternal damnation!"

This belief has become so culturally acceptable that even "evangelicals" have embraced it. They refer to it as "Evangelical Universalism" (EU). However, to separate their brand of universalism from the version of the secularists, they have "Christianized" it. They have done this by adding the stipulation that all will be saved after they suffer for a while—*to pay the price for their sins*. Therefore, those who hold this view are denying the sufficiency of the death of Jesus to pay the price for all the sins of the world.

Both forms of universalism refuse to consider the social/psychological requirement for a final and just judgment. Let us consider some of the reasons for the absolute necessity of an ultimate judgment:

1. Universalism implies that God doesn't care very much about cruelty and injustice. And if He doesn't care, why should we? Why should society have courts and punishments if being non-punitive ultimately trumps everything else? Some might argue that it is expedient to have courts and punishments even if the question of justice is irrelevant. However, punishment without justice isn't just, and no society will long survive such a system. Even the martyred saints in the presence of God cry out for justice:

> They cried out with a loud voice, "O Sovereign
> Lord, holy and true, how long before you will
> judge and avenge our blood on those who dwell on
> the earth?" Then they were each given a white robe
> and told to rest a little longer, until the number of
> their fellow servants and their brothers should be
> complete, who were to be killed as they themselves
> had been.
>
> REVELATION 6:10-11

These martyrs were thus divinely affirmed regarding their desire for justice. We also, having been created in the likeness of God, have a deeply imbedded desire to see justice.

2. A final judgment gives us the freedom to love others. For when we have such a mind-set, we can commit our concerns and longings for ultimate justice to God. We can devote ourselves to love, knowing that someday God will punish—and with the utmost justice. Not having experienced radical victimization for the most part, we Westerners have become quite comfortable. We fail to fully appreciate the fact that the imposition of justice brings psychological closure to our minds and emotions. We are thus enabled to move on.

> Beloved, never avenge yourselves, but leave it to
> the wrath of God, for it is written, "Vengeance is
> mine, I will repay, says the Lord." To the contrary,
> "if your enemy is hungry, feed him; if he is thirsty,
> give him something to drink … "
>
> ROMANS 12:19–20

3. A final judgment provides the necessary warning that we are accountable, not only for following the statutes of the State, but also for following the dictates of our own conscience. Contrary to this, those who believe in EU are granting moral license since, at the end of the day, "There will be no consequences for our actions or attitudes. Nothing we do will be ultimately judgable or condemnable. Questions of right and wrong will be swept away by God's love for all humanity." Instead, this is what Scripture has to say:

> For this is the will of God, your sanctification ... that no one transgress and wrong his brother in this matter, because the Lord is an avenger in all these things, as we told you beforehand and solemnly warned you.
>
> 1 THESSALONIANS 4:3A, 6

4. Universalism provides the affluent, self-indulgent, myopic West with the ultimate "designer" gods who tell us: "Live as you like. Far be it from me to interfere with your fulfillment and pleasure. No matter how you live, it will all be wonderful in the end." This fabrication disposes of the question of justice in favor of our immediate comforts and proclivities. However, we need to ask ourselves if our disgust with the idea of eternal judgment is a product of reason and evidence—or merely the outworking of a skewed moral compass.

> [Scoffers] will say, "Where is the promise of his coming? For ever since the fathers fell asleep, all things are continuing as they were from the beginning of creation." For they deliberately overlook this fact, that the heavens existed long ago, and the earth was formed out of water and through water by the word of God, and that by means of these the world that then existed was deluged with water and perished.
>
> 2 PETER 3:4–6

5. Eternal punishment guards against an entitlement mentality. For example, "public assistance" is granted as an entitlement; those who receive it are "entitled" to it. And what good have these entitlements accomplished? Respected economists have admitted that our entitlement programs, for the most part, have damaged nearly all those who have received their mis-guided largesse. Instead of gratefulness, the recipients become convinced that they *deserve* what they receive. In much the same way, universalism conveys the wrong and damaging idea that we are *entitled* to God's love. We are no more entitled to God's love than your cat is entitled to a yearly excursion to the French Riviera. God does not love

us because we deserve it, but because *He wants to love us.* Jesus warned that we must regard ourselves as unworthy of the blessings of God:

> "So you also, when you have done all that you were commanded, say, 'We are unworthy servants; we have only done what was our duty.'"
>
> LUKE 17:10

Granted, the idea of a "God of judgment" may not conjure up the most comforting image, but perhaps this is the very God we need.

The highest importance should be given to the abundance of Scriptural evidence against the eventual salvation of all.

> "And many of them that sleep in the dust of the earth shall awake, some to everlasting life, and some to shame and *everlasting contempt.*"
>
> DANIEL 12:2 KJV, *italics mine*

> "And whosoever shall speak a word against the Son of man, it shall be forgiven him; but whosoever shall speak against the Holy Spirit, *it shall not be forgiven him*, neither in this world, nor in that which is to come."
>
> MATTHEW 12:32 ASV, *italics mine*

> "And these shall go away into *eternal punishment*: but the righteous into eternal life."
>
> MATTHEW 25:46 ASV, *italics mine*

> "Strive to enter through the narrow door. *For many, I tell you, will seek to enter and will not be able.*"
>
> LUKE 13:24, *italics mine*

> "Whoever believes in the Son has eternal life, but *whoever rejects the Son will not* ["never" ESV] *see life*, for God's wrath remains on him."
>
> JOHN 3:36 NIV, *italics mine*

Or do you not know that *the unrighteous will not inherit the kingdom of God?* Do not be deceived: neither the sexually immoral, nor idolaters, nor adulterers, nor men who practice homosexuality, nor thieves, nor the greedy, nor drunkards, nor revilers, nor swindlers will inherit the kingdom of God.

1 CORINTHIANS 6:9–10, italics mine

... I warn you, as I warned you before, that *those who do such things will not inherit the kingdom of God.*

GALATIANS 5:21, italics mine

For you may be sure of this, that everyone who is sexually immoral or impure, or who is covetous (that is, an idolater), has *no inheritance in the kingdom of Christ and God.*

EPHESIANS 5:5, italics mine

... but if it beareth thorns and thistles, it is rejected and nigh unto a curse; *whose end is to be burned.*

HEBREWS 6:8 ASV, italics mine

Even as Sodom and Gomorrah, and the cities about them, having in like manner with these given themselves over to fornication and gone after strange flesh, are set forth as an example, *suffering the punishment of eternal fire.*

JUDE 1:7 ASV, italics mine

... wild waves of the sea, foaming out their own shame; wandering stars, *for whom the blackness of darkness hath been reserved for ever.*

JUDE 1:13 ASV, italics mine

... if any man shall take away from the words of the book of this prophecy, *God shall take away his part from the tree of life,* and out of the holy city, which are written in this book.

REVELATION 22:19 ASV, italics mine

"For I say unto you, that except your righteousness shall exceed the righteousness of the scribes and Pharisees, *ye shall in no wise enter into the kingdom of heaven.*"

MATTHEW 5:20 ASV, italics mine

In view of these verses, those who espouse evangelical universalism are offering a false and deceptive hope.

They cannot offer a single verse that claims that all will be saved after they experience a temporary punishment for their sins. Nevertheless, they present many verses that *seem to say* that all will eventually be saved. However, each of the verses they use fails to explicitly say this. For example:

> … so that at the name of Jesus every knee should bow, in heaven and on earth and under the earth, and every tongue confess that Jesus Christ is Lord, to the glory of God the Father.
>
> PHILIPPIANS 2:10–11
> *see also Romans 14:10-12*

Does this mean that all will be saved? Isaiah also seems to suggest a universal salvation:

> "I have sworn by myself, The word is gone out of my mouth in righteousness, and shall not return, That unto me every knee shall bow, Every tongue shall swear. Surely, shall one say, in the LORD have I righteousness and strength: Even to him shall men come; And all that are incensed against him shall be ashamed. In the LORD shall all the seed of Israel be justified, and shall glory."
>
> ISAIAH 45:23–25 KJV

However, even if these verses point to a universal salvation, they refer only to those who are left alive at the end of this age:

> Then everyone who survives of all the nations that have come against Jerusalem shall go up year after year to worship the King, the LORD of hosts, and to keep the Feast of Booths.
>
> ZECHARIAH 14:16

> It shall come to pass in the latter days that the mountain of the house of the LORD shall be established as the highest of the mountains, and shall be lifted up above the hills; and all the nations shall flow to it, and many peoples shall

come, and say: "Come, let us go up to the mountain of the LORD, to the house of the God of Jacob, that he may teach us his ways and that we may walk in his paths." For out of Zion shall go forth the law, and the word of the LORD from Jerusalem. He shall judge between the nations, and shall decide disputes for many peoples; and they shall beat their swords into plowshares, and their spears into pruning hooks; nation shall not lift up sword against nation, neither shall they learn war anymore.

ISAIAH 2:2–4; MICAH 4:1-3

The New Testament also refers to a great salvation at the end among those who remain:

For if their [Israel's] rejection means the reconciliation of the world, what will their acceptance mean but life from the dead?

ROMANS 11:15

There will be a great salvation at the time of Jesus' return, but this falls far short of universalism's claims. EU also cite this verse:

For in him all the fullness of God was pleased to dwell, and through him [Jesus] *to reconcile to himself all things*, whether on earth or in heaven, making peace by the blood of his cross.

COLOSSIANS 1:19-20, *italics mine*

" ... to reconcile to himself all things" could mean many different things, even perhaps including the annihilation of some, or the isolation of others.

However, evangelical universalists never cite the following passage:

And you, who once were alienated and hostile in mind, doing evil deeds, he has now reconciled in his body of flesh by his death, in order to present you holy and blameless and above reproach before him, *if indeed you continue in the faith*, stable and steadfast, not shifting from the hope of the gospel that you heard ...

COLOSSIANS 1:21-23A, *italics mine*

Paul was addressing people in the church and warning them that they must continue in the faith. This is a "condition," or caveat, that EU refuses to recognize.

Nevertheless, evangelical universalists are quick to cite the following passage which claims that Christ is in all:

> Do not lie to one another, seeing that you have put off the old self with its practices and have put on the new self, which is being renewed in knowledge after the image of its creator. Here [in Christ] there is not Greek and Jew, circumcised and uncircumcised, barbarian, Scythian, slave, free; *but Christ is all, and in all.*
>
> COLOSSIANS 3:9-11, *italics mine*

However, the context makes it clear that Paul was not referring to all the world ... but *to all the Church.* This is precisely what the next verse in the same passage indicates:

> Put on then, *as God's chosen ones,* holy and beloved, compassionate hearts, kindness, humility, meekness, and patience.
>
> COLOSSIANS 3:12, *italics mine*

But not everyone in the world is a part of the family of God's chosen ones, to be sure:

> Do not be unequally yoked with unbelievers. For what partnership has righteousness with lawlessness? Or what fellowship has light with darkness? What accord has Christ with Belial? Or what portion does a believer share with an unbeliever? What agreement has the temple of God with idols?
>
> 2 CORINTHIANS 6:14-16

Here is one last verse which EU cites:

> For as *in Adam all die,* so also *in Christ shall all be made alive.*
>
> 1 CORINTHIANS 15:21–25, *italics mine*

Those "in Adam" die. We were all in Adam; therefore, we all experience death. However, we are not all "in Christ." The evangelical universalist would most likely disagree. But does his stance accord with the following passage of Scripture?

> But each in his own order: Christ the firstfruits, then at his coming *those who belong to Christ.* Then comes the end, when he delivers the kingdom to God the Father after destroying every rule and every authority and power. For he must reign *until he has put all his enemies under his feet.*
>
> 1 CORINTHIANS 15:23-25, *italics mine*

It seems clear that those "in Christ" are "those who belong to Christ." In sharp contrast, "his enemies" will be put "under His feet." This is hardly a description of salvation.

Conclusion

Evangelical universalism represents the undermining of the entire biblical revelation. Why evangelize if everyone is to be saved? Just let them have their fun, right? Why study the Bible, pray, or live obediently if all will eventually be saved? EU detracts from everything that the Bible teaches. Consequently, the Bible is rendered almost irrelevant.

Another claim of EU is that eternal punishment, whether it is eternal death or torment, denies that God is love. However, this is clearly not what the Bible teaches about love. Indeed, God loves His creation (Psalm 145:15) and cares for it. However, there is nothing in the Bible that says that God loves the devil and his demons. They have become corrupt and no longer resemble God's original creation.

Furthermore, it is possible to reach a point in our lives when we have corrupted ourselves so entirely that God cuts us loose to follow our own desires:

> They are darkened in their understanding, alienated from the life of God because of the ignorance that is in them, due to their hardness of heart. They have become callous and have given themselves up to sensuality, greedy to practice every kind of impurity.
>
> EPHESIANS 4:18–19
> *see also Romans 1:24-28*

Is God under any obligation to continue to love those who have utterly and continually rejected Him? Of course not! Instead, He has promised to receive all who come to Him (Romans 10:12-13). King David had committed adultery with a married woman and then had her faithful husband killed to cover up his sins. Later, he made this confession to God:

> I acknowledged my sin to you, and I did not cover my iniquity; I said, "I will confess my transgressions to the LORD," and you forgave the iniquity of my sin.
>
> PSALM 32:5

To show that He had forgiven David, God chose his son Solomon—the product of an illicit relationship—to be the next king of Israel. God is willing to receive any who come to Him and genuinely confess his or her sins.

How can we blame God for His supposed "lack of love"? How can we blame Him if we too insist on an apology in order to be reconciled with a friend who has continued to steal from us, malign our character, and destroy our reputation? God asks of us no more than a sincere confession of sins (Jeremiah 3:11-13; 1 John 1:8-9).

It is also very possible that the unbeliever—who hates God in this life— would continue to hate Him even more in the life to come. After all, in the next life the unbeliever would be confronted with God's unremitting, exposing light. The Bible seems to suggest that such a person would flee from His presence, even if it led to a place of torment:

> For God did not send his Son into the world to condemn the world, but in order that the world might be saved through him. Whoever believes in him is not condemned, but whoever does not believe is condemned already, because he has not believed in the name of the only Son of God. And this is the judgment: the light has come into the world, and people loved the darkness rather than the light because their works were evil. For everyone who does wicked things hates the light and does not come to the light, lest his works should be exposed.
>
> JOHN 3:17-20

GOD AND EVIL

CHAPTER 8

Is Eternal Torment Unjust?

Perhaps the most serious charge brought against the righteousness of God is the accusation that eternal punishment is unjust. It doesn't seem fair that God would punish eternally for wrongs that have been committed in this life. The famous atheist Robert Ingersoll (1833-1899) was particularly robust in his indictment of any god who would condemn some to eternal punishment:

> "The doctrine of eternal punishment is the infamy of infamies. As I have often said, the man who believes in eternal torment, in the justice of endless pain, is suffering from at least two diseases—petrifaction of the heart and putrefaction of the brain."[1]

This perspective is part of an even broader challenge—the problem of evil and suffering. The position is often presented in the following way:

> *If the God of the Bible is just, loving, and omnipotent, he wouldn't allow the death of babies and suffering in general.*

Put less crudely, the atheistic argument goes like this:

- *PREMISE #1:* Eternal punishment is not just.

- *PREMISE #2:* The God of the Bible promises eternal punishment.

- *CONCLUSION:* The God of the Bible cannot be just (or even exist).

PREMISE #1
Eternal punishment is not just.

Admittedly, this challenge is difficult to address. For one thing, it is hard to nail down in a precise manner the nature of eternal punishment. Skeptics charge that they will not believe in a God who is stoking the eternal fires of hell. Even supposedly Christian evolutionists question the just nature of the God of the Bible. For example, the former co-head of the Biologos Foundation, which is devoted to promoting evolution to the Church, quoted Richard Dawkins and seemed to affirm what the world-famous atheist had said:

> [The Old Testament God is a] " ... tyrannical anthropomorphic deity... [who] commanded the Jews to go on genocidal rampages" ... But who believes in this [Old Testament] deity any more, besides those same fundamentalists who think the earth is 10,000 years old? Modern theology has moved past this view of God.[2]

Although Karl Giberson didn't mention his disdain for eternal punishment, it seems likely that his preference for "modern theology" would also lead him and many other "Christian" evolutionists to question the New Testament teachings on eternal punishment.

Can the skeptic coherently say that eternal punishment is unjust? To claim that something is unjust, we need to compare it with an objective standard of justice. However, skeptics have rejected an objective standard in favor of moral relativism. They have become like the math teacher who grades an exam without the benefit of any objectively correct answers. To do this would be absurd. However, this is exactly what the skeptic does when he claims that eternal punishment is unjust.

As an atheist, C. S. Lewis saw this glaring contradiction:

> My argument against God was that the universe seemed so cruel and unjust. But how had I got this idea of "just" and "unjust"? ... What was I comparing this universe with when I called it unjust? ... Of course I could have given up my idea of justice by saying it was nothing but a private idea of my own. But if I did that, then my argument against

God collapsed too—for the argument depended on saying that the world was really [objectively] unjust, not simply that it did not happen to please my private fancies... Consequently atheism turns out to be too simple.[3]

Lacking an objective standard of justice, Lewis perceived that atheism is unable to charge God, or anyone else, with injustice.

The poet and atheist, W. H. Auden, learned the same lesson—that secular humanism is unable to provide any moral basis for our indignation against evil. Auden moved to Germantown in New York City from his home in Ireland in the early 1930s. While he was watching a news clip in the movie theater about the Nazi invasion of Poland, he was horrified to see the audience rise to its feet, applauding and crying out, "Destroy the Poles!" Auden wanted to take a strong moral stance against their response, but he couldn't. He began to recognize that, as an atheist, his values were merely self-constructed. Therefore, they lacked any authority to make a moral claim. This realization sent him into a moral tailspin. After his crisis of faith, Auden came to understand that there was indeed a God who provided an objective standard of justice. He became a Christian.

Does the skeptic have any substantive and objective basis for his indignation against the prospect of eternal judgment? Seemingly not.

Rather than being unjust, it seems that eternal punishment might be an essential component of justice. As the Apostle Peter argued, eternal punishment was also implemented to serve as a deterrent:

> For if God did not spare angels when they sinned, but cast them into hell and committed them to chains of gloomy darkness to be kept until the judgment; if he did not spare the ancient world, but preserved Noah, a herald of righteousness, with seven others, when he brought a flood upon the world of the ungodly; if by turning the cities of Sodom and Gomorrah to ashes he condemned them to extinction, making them an example of what is going to happen to the ungodly; and if he rescued righteous Lot, greatly distressed by the sensual conduct of the wicked... then the Lord knows how to rescue the godly

from trials, and to keep the unrighteous under punishment
until the day of judgment.

2 PETER 2:4–7, 9

Contrary to secular opinion, we need to know that God will ultimately judge. It is this knowledge that enables us to leave aside thoughts of revenge, hatred, and unforgiveness. Instead, we can apply ourselves to what we have been called to do—love.

Miroslav Volf, who survived the civil wars of the former Yugoslavia, has written:

> The only means of prohibiting all recourses to violence by ourselves is to insist that violence is legitimate only when it comes from God ... My thesis [is] that the practice of non-violence requires a belief in divine vengeance.[4]

Volf knew that his stance would be unpopular in the West. He understood that if we have no substantive experience with victimization, then we will also have no experience with the overwhelming, life-controlling need to avenge.

Writer and theologian, Tim Keller, explains:

> Can our passion for justice be honored in a way that does not nurture our desire for blood and vengeance? Volf says the best resource for this is a belief in the concept of God's divine justice. If I don't believe that there is a God who will eventually put all things right, I will take up the sword and will be sucked into the endless vortex of retaliation. Only if I am sure that there's a God who will right all wrongs and settle all accounts perfectly do I have the power to refrain.[5]

Instead of the perspective that the belief in the existence of hell leads to a more hellish society, it seems that the absence of this belief would incline us to seek our own form of "justice." The impulse to seek justice transcends the way we have been raised. Even children—universally—demand justice. Desiring justice is part of our human nature, and it demands expression and satisfaction.

Keller observes that in societies where the doctrine of eternal judgment is rejected, brutality reigns:

> Many people complain that belief in a God of judgment will lead to a more brutal society ... [but] in both Nazism and Communism ... a loss of belief in a God of judgment can lead to brutality. If we are free to shape life and morals any way we choose without ultimate accountability, it can lead to violence. Volf and [poet Czeslaw] Milosz argue that the doctrine of God's final judgment is a necessary undergirding for human practices of love and peacemaking.[6]

The threat of eternal judgment seems to be a necessary element for a thriving society, as long as that judgment is associated with the possibility of forgiveness.

PREMISE #2

The God of the Bible promises eternal punishment.

To deal properly with this issue, we need to survey the entirety of the Bible's teachings on the subject. Does God proactively torment unbelievers with fire? I doubt it. It seems that much of the language of eternal fire is figurative rather than literal. For example, sometimes Jesus refers to hell as "outer darkness":

> "Then the king told the attendants, 'Tie him hand and foot, and throw him outside, into the darkness, where there will be weeping and gnashing of teeth.'"
>
> MATTHEW 22:13
> *see also Matthew 8:12; 25:13*
> *"the fiery furnace" is mentioned in Matthew 13:42, 50*

Clearly, both the language of eternal fire and outer darkness cannot be taken literally. After all, they are mutually exclusive—a fire emanates light, not darkness. Besides that, the verses mentioning eternal judgment as "the weeping and gnashing of teeth" are associated with neither fire nor darkness, but with eternal regret:

> "There will be weeping there, and gnashing of teeth, when you see Abraham, Isaac and Jacob and all the prophets in the kingdom of God, but you yourselves thrown out."
>
> LUKE 13:28

In this verse, "weeping...and gnashing of teeth" is not the product of darkness or fire but of the eternal loss of blessing. This would lead us to believe that eternal torment might not be the product of God proactively afflicting these unfortunate souls. Rather, the perception and realization of their immense loss is more likely indicated.

To complicate the matter further, eternal punishment is also referred to as "destruction":

> "And do not fear those who kill the body but cannot kill the soul. Rather fear him [God] who can destroy both soul and body in hell."
>
> MATTHEW 10:28
> *see also 2 Thessalonians 1:9 and James 4:12*

In view of these uncertainties, the charges against God and an adequate defense for God's justice become difficult or even impossible to make.

In addition, it also seems unjust for God to punish all the lost souls with the same exact punishment. Instead, it is apparent that there will be degrees of punishment:

> Then Jesus began to denounce the cities in which most of his miracles had been performed, because they did not repent. "Woe to you, Korazin! Woe to you, Bethsaida! If the miracles that were performed in you had been performed in Tyre and Sidon, they would have repented long ago in sackcloth and ashes. But I tell you, it will be more bearable for Tyre and Sidon on the day of judgment than for you."
>
> MATTHEW 11:20-22

It seems that the judgment meted out to us will depend upon the amount of evidence we have been given (John 15:22, 24). Nevertheless, we all have some degree of evidence—or light— according to Romans 1:18-20 and 2:14-15. In any case, we reject God's light in favor of the darkness of ignorance (John 3:19-21).

In addition to these daunting uncertainties, we are only given hints about the fate of those who are stillborn, or of those who are aborted. Once again, it seems as if one's judgment will coincide with one's understanding and actions:

> "That servant who knows his master's will and does not get ready or does not do what his master wants will be beaten with many blows. But the one who does not know and does things deserving punishment will be beaten with few blows. From everyone who has been given much, much will be demanded; and from the one who has been entrusted with much, much more will be asked."
>
> LUKE 12:47-48

Although these verses do not explicitly lay out the punishment that each one deserves, they do teach that God will judge fairly and will consider each individual case.

~

There are also other considerations that make it difficult for us to determine the exact nature of eternal punishment. For example, it seems very possible that hell and our condemnation might be self-chosen:

> "For God did not send his Son into the world to condemn the world, but to save the world through him. Whoever believes in him is not condemned, but whoever does not believe stands condemned already because he has not believed in the name of God's one and only Son. This is the verdict ["condemnation" in the KJV]: Light has come into the world, but men loved darkness instead of light because their deeds were evil. Everyone who does evil hates the light, and will not come into the light for fear that his deeds will be exposed."
>
> JOHN 3:17-20

Many verses inform us that Jesus didn't come to judge. For a sampling of just some of those verses, we have John 5:45; 8:15; 12:47-49; and Matthew 7:2. How then is the unbeliever condemned? It seems likely that he is self-condemned! How can this be? "Whoever does not believe stands condemned already because he has not believed [or, he has refused to believe] (John 3:18)." Immediately thereafter, verse 19 reconfirms that judgment is a self-judgment. The unbeliever has the light but rejects the light in favor of the darkness. He flees from the light, lest he be exposed. This means that, ultimately, we get what we want—either we remain eternally in the presence of the light—or we flee from it. What could be more just?

Will this same condemnation accompany the unbeliever into the next life, before the great judgment? It seems so. There are many other verses assuring us that those who reject the light will not approach the light, but flee:

> In that day mankind will cast away their idols of silver and their idols of gold, which they made for themselves to worship, to the moles and to the bats, to enter the caverns of the rocks and the clefts of the cliffs, from before the terror of the LORD, and from the splendor of his majesty, when he rises to terrify the earth.
>
> ISAIAH 2:20–21
> *see also Psalm 1:4-5, 15:1-2, 24:3-4; Malachi 3:2;*
> *Luke 21:36; Revelation 6:15-16, 20:11*

It is very possible that this same hatred of the light—the sinner's present self-condemnation—will also bring about self-condemnation in the next life. Although this might be horrific for us to comprehend, we cannot easily charge God with injustice. Instead, it is we who are unjust! From this perspective, the sinner is merely choosing his own destiny—the darkness in which he feels the greatest sense of comfort. How can this be unjust?

But doesn't this theory circumvent the Bible's teachings that "we must all appear before the judgment seat of Christ, that each one may receive what is due him for the things done while in the body, whether good or bad" (2 Corinthians 5:10)? No! The great judgment might simply represent an affirmation, a rubber-stamping, of what we have already chosen.

For the children of God, the great judgment will be a time of rejoicing. This is because our fate will already have been settled. It is then that we will be changed, "in a twinkling of an eye" (1 Corinthians 15:50-52), to become like Him (1 John 3:2 and 1 Thessalonians 4:14-17). Therefore, when we stand before Him, there will be no doubt about our eternal fate.

Likewise, it seems that the lover-of-darkness has also sealed his own fate by running from the light. In view of this possibility, no one can coherently blame God.

However, doesn't an eternal punishment, even if it is self-chosen, still call into question God's justice? Not necessarily. Perhaps God will give the sufferers the option to pull-the-plug and face utter annihilation. Although there isn't a verse that precludes this possibility, there are no verses that teach that God will provide this option. This is just another way of saying that there is much uncertainty about hell. In any event, if God is the giver of life, there would be nothing unjust about His allowing the self-condemned the choice to extinguish their lives.

Nevertheless, the prospect of hell is dreadful. The Bible consistently warns that the punishment is eternal, whether that means eternal death, fire, or darkness:

> "Then they will go away to eternal punishment, but the righteous to eternal life."
>
> MATTHEW 25:46

The span of the punishment will be just as eternal as "eternal life." It is understandable that such verses are troubling. However, we do not know the exact nature of this eternal judgment. Considering this uncertainty, the lover-of-light will give God the benefit of the doubt, while those who hate the light will find reasons to negate its existence. Therefore, I often respond to these challenges in this way:

> *I don't know how it will all come out in the end, but I do know that our God is both merciful and just. I also believe that our Creator has the right to judge His creation. If we find this troubling, we should reconcile with Him before it is too late.*

CONCLUSION:
The God of the Bible cannot be just (or even exist).

Job had also charged God with injustice, and it seemed that he had good reason to do so. God had allowed Satan to deprive him of almost everything, and Job was left devastated. However, his loss didn't justify Job's allegations against God.

> Then the LORD answered Job out of the storm. He said: "Who is this that darkens my counsel with words without knowledge? Brace yourself like a man; I will question you, and you shall answer me."
>
> JOB 38:1-3

The Lord then asked Job an extensive set of questions, and Job could not answer any of them. Job got the point. His meager understanding forbade him from bringing indictments against God. Therefore, he repented:

> The LORD said to Job: "Will the one who contends with the Almighty correct him? Let him who accuses God answer him!" Then Job answered the LORD: "I am unworthy—how can I reply to you? I put my hand over my mouth."
>
> JOB 40:1-4

What made Job unworthy? He was beginning to understand that he had spoken presumptuously about things he did not understand:

> "You [God] asked, 'Who is this that obscures my counsel without knowledge?' Surely I spoke of things I did not understand, things too wonderful for me to know. You [God] said, 'Listen now, and I will speak; I will question you, and you shall answer me.' My ears had heard of you but now my eyes have seen you. Therefore I despise myself and repent in dust and ashes."
>
> JOB 42:3-6

Many will find Job's response repugnant, but why? We too speak about things we do not understand. Although we might know that we are just a speck in this grand universe, we act as if we were nearly omniscient. Yet, we cannot even define the basics—the nature of time, space, matter, or light. The simplest things are beyond our knowing, and yet there are some who have the hubris to accuse God of injustice. Like Job, perhaps we too need to learn a little humility in keeping with our cosmic insignificance.

⁓

If eternal punishment is a reality, then love requires us to warn. The greater the threat, the greater the need for warning. This is especially true regarding eternal punishment. In the West, we readily dismiss this threat as so barbaric that it couldn't possibly be the design of a God of love. However, if this is our mind-set, then we are refusing to consider how little we truly understand.

Tim Keller calls hell "simply one's chosen identity."[6] In other words, hell is something we choose. C. S. Lewis calls hell "the greatest monument to human freedom." In *The Great Divorce*, he paints a vivid picture of how we choose hell:

> Hell begins with a grumbling mood, always complaining, always blaming others ... but you are still distinct from it. You may even criticize it in yourself and wish you could stop it. But there may come a day when you can no longer. Then there will be no you left to criticize the mood or even to enjoy it, but just the grumble itself, going on forever like a machine. It is not a question of God "sending us" to hell. In each of us there is something growing, which will be hell unless it is nipped in the bud.[7]

How then do we "nip it in the bud"? By confessing our sins (1 John 1:9) and crying out for Christ's mercy (Romans 10:12-13)!

How did we get into this mess? According to Lewis, we continue to harden our heart against the Lord until we have no heart left (Romans 1:24-28). With every refusal to turn away from our sins and turn to Christ, we embrace our final destiny. Lewis therefore concludes:

> There are only two kinds of people—those who say "Thy will be done" to God or those to whom God in the end says, "Thy will be done." All that are in Hell choose it.[8]

Is this assessment biblical? Keller correctly reflects that there are no biblical accounts of people pleading to be released from hell into God's presence (Luke 16). This makes perfect biblical sense. If we hate the light in this life, we will flee it as well when we are confronted with its greater intensity in the next life (John 3:19-21).

The Apostle Paul taught that we are a stench to those who are perishing (2 Corinthians 2:14-16). How much more will our Lord's glorious presence nauseate those who refused the light in this life—when they arrive in the one to come! By that time, their fate is sealed, along with their tastes and preferences.

This is horrific. What then must we do if we love the hell-bound? Once again, we must warn!

~

The skeptic will object that if God is omnipotent, he should have been able to achieve his "loving" purposes without a hell. However, the omnipotence of God is often misunderstood. Although God can do anything He wants to do, he cannot do it in absolutely any way.

Jesus prayed that there might have been another way for His Father to accomplish His redemptive purposes, apart from the Cross:

> And going a little farther he fell on his face and prayed, saying, "My Father, if it be possible, let this cup pass from me; nevertheless, not as I will, but as you will."
>
> MATTHEW 26:39

Evidently, there was no other way. This illustrates that God is indeed limited in the ways He can accomplish what He wants to do. In fact, He has many limitations: He cannot sin; nor can He violate His promises or His character. Furthermore, logic might also be a part of His character. If this is so, He might not be free to entertain within His mind another logical "operating system" that does not coincide with the one that He originally set in place.

If we are willing to acknowledge this possibility, it might help us to accept and even to be at peace with some of the questions that we cannot answer with our limited understanding. For example:

- *"Why couldn't God create a world without suffering or eternal punishment?"*
- *"Why did He create people whom He knew would reject Him?"*
- *"If He is all powerful, why does He not save all?"*

Perhaps His righteous nature requires Him to punish. Perhaps He allows some to go beyond even His ability to save:

> He who is often reproved, yet stiffens his neck, will
> suddenly be *broken beyond healing*.
>
> PROVERBS 29:1, *italics mine*

I cannot claim to have satisfying answers to these questions. In fact, for me, they only provoke more questions. But I have come to accept this state of affairs. I trust that my God had good reasons for creating the universe as He did. There are just some things within that universe that I simply cannot fathom.

CHAPTER 9

Do We Need the Wrath of God?

The idea of God as a "cosmic watchdog" who will punish us is entirely unacceptable to Western thinking. Instead, men and women in Western societies insist on being the captains of their own ships. Therefore, the idea of having an *uber-captain* is repugnant to them.

Fully aware of this repugnance and eager to cater to the tastes of the prevailing society, the Church in the West has grown conveniently silent about a God of wrath. He is now presented exclusively as a God of love. In *Noborderland: Finding Amazing Grace in a Dark and Dying World*, Tom Graffagnino has appropriately written:

> The coddled Western church of bright lights and high
> performance has hit a snag. Social and cultural "relevance"
> has elbowed holiness, righteousness, and repentance off
> the auditorium stage. The gospel of grace and the necessary
> bad news that must necessarily precede it have become
> increasingly and noticeably absent in our comfort-driven,
> "Me first," "Me Too," and "Have it Your Way" world.[1]

Consequently, the Church has largely rejected the fire-and-brimstone message. But should it be this way? For some, the highest expression of love requires us to make others feel comfortable. After all, no one wants to feel condemned by an unsettling sermon. But what if our comfortable lives have insulated us from the truths of God? What if we are being insulated even from the truths that would lead us to our spiritual well-being? Citing Michael Horton, Graffagnino claims that this is the very thing that has been happening:

> We must be stripped of our fig leaves in order to be clothed
> with Christ's righteousness so we can stand in the judgment
> of a holy God. The question is whether the aim of ministry
> today is to tear off our fig leaves so we can be clothed with
> Christ or to help us add a few more.[2]

Sadly, much of ministry today is aimed at making us feel more comfortable about ourselves. The Gospel is relegated to a position of secondary importance. Instead, according to Grafagnino, preaching must embrace "tough love." For that is the only way that we might enter God's love. The preaching of the Gospel must serve as a "double-edged sword." One side of the sword penetrates to the core of our sin and rebellion. And that enables us to experience the other side—the offer of real comfort, the comfort of knowing Christ.

Must we first understand and perhaps even taste the wrath of God before we can appreciate the rescue of God—His great sacrifice to bring us into an eternal relationship of love? Must we first understand from what we have been saved in order for us to fully appreciate what we have been saved to? Without this dual understanding, the Gospel will continue to be considered foolish by the unspiritual (1 Corinthians 2:14). In fact, the message of the Gospel is counted as foolishness by all who do not regularly feed upon the Word. For in the Scriptures, we find the truths that are inherent in both the wrath and the rescue of God.

The reality of God's wrath elucidates many needful truths:

God's wrath upon Jesus informs us of His love in a more profound way than anything else could.

For several years, I had undergone such horrendous suffering that I couldn't shake the idea that God might be a deceiving sadist who had created us for His perverse entertainment. However, the revelation of Jesus taking upon Himself the wrath that we all deserved finally convinced me otherwise. Jesus' horrible death on the Cross proved that God could not be a sadist or a master deceiver. Such people would never sacrifice themselves for anyone else:

> ... but God shows his love for us in that while we were
> still sinners, Christ died for us. Since, therefore, we have
> now been justified by his blood, much more shall we be
> saved by him from the wrath of God. For if while we were
> enemies we were reconciled to God by the death of his
> Son, much more, now that we are reconciled, shall we be
> saved by his life.
>
> ROMANS 5:8-10

God's wrath serves as a poignant declaration and reminder that He detests sin and must punish it.

His intolerance of sin is so great that He could not even endure being
near Israel, despite His love for her (Numbers 20:16). Instead, He had to
send His Messenger to lead Israel:

> "I will send an angel before you, and I will drive out the
> Canaanites, the Amorites, the Hittites, the Perizzites, the
> Hivites, and the Jebusites. Go up to a land flowing with
> milk and honey; but I will not go up among you, lest I
> consume you on the way, for you are a stiff-necked people."
>
> EXODUS 33:2-3

We might wonder why God would choose to act this way. There is only
one possible answer: this is His nature, and we must accept this fact. His
righteous nature had to be satisfied through the punishment for sin. He
had to convincingly demonstrate to us His absolute abhorrence of it:

> ... for all have sinned and fall short of the glory of
> God, and are justified by his grace as a gift, through the
> redemption that is in Christ Jesus, whom God put forward
> as a propitiation by his blood, to be received by faith. *This
> was to show God's righteousness,* because in his divine
> forbearance he had passed over former sins. *It was to show
> his righteousness* at the present time, so that he might be
> just and the justifier of the one who has faith in Jesus.
>
> ROMANS 3:23-26, *italics mine*

God had been patient with our unpunished sins. The ultimate sin offering of His Son not only demonstrated God's love and propitiated—satisfied—His nature, but it also demonstrated His severe righteousness. All this was done through Jesus' death on the Cross. Therefore, although His forgiveness is limitless, we can see with the utmost clarity that any sin is detestable before God. We, therefore, literally need to fear God as we entertain any sinful thoughts, and maybe especially any proud, seductive thoughts. Thus, the wrath and righteousness of God are necessary for our well-being, in the same way that the fear of falling off the edge of a building is also necessary.

It has been argued that, if God is all-powerful, He should have been able to forgive us without "killing" His Son. However, God is not robotic. Once again, our righteous God has a nature by which He must live. And that righteous nature requires satisfaction—propitiation and atonement—for sin.

If this sounds unreasonable, just imagine a friend saying to you, "Whenever I see yellow flowers, it fills me with anxiety." You might think that this is petty. You might even try to explain it away as merely a biochemical reaction, but this would entirely miss the point. The fact remains—she feels anxious at the sight of yellow flowers. Therefore, buying her yellow flowers would understandably be regarded as callous. In light of this, we must accept this about our friend. If we are willing to accept our friend's feelings and limitations, *how much more must we accept our immutable God's self-disclosure that He must punish sin?*

If God's wrath is real, people need to be warned:

> Put to death therefore what is earthly in you: sexual immorality, impurity, passion, evil desire, and covetousness, which is idolatry. On account of these the wrath of God is coming.
>
> COLOSSIANS 3:5-6
> *see also Ephesians 5:6 and 1 Corinthians 6:7-11*

It also seems that we already have an intuitive knowledge of God's wrath, even if we choose to deny it:

Though they know God's righteous decree that those who practice such things deserve to die, they not only do them but give approval to those who practice them.

ROMANS 1:32

If we didn't have this knowledge of God's wrath, we would simply be able to laugh-off such a "fairy tale." But instead, humanity hates God because men and women correctly sense that they deserve His wrath. In spite of this awareness, they suppress it with many forms of self-promotion and self-deceit.

The threat of God's wrath promotes reform.

King Josiah had been ignorant of the Lord until the *Book of the Law* had been found and brought to him. He therefore directed his priests:

"Go, inquire of the LORD for me, and for the people, and for all Judah, concerning the words of this book that has been found. For great is the wrath of the LORD that is kindled against us, because our fathers have not obeyed the words of this book, to do according to all that is written concerning us."

2 KINGS 22:13

The knowledge of God's wrath resulted in great reforms (Ezekiel 22:20-22).

God's wrath is also just and freeing:

... since indeed *God considers it just to repay with affliction those who afflict you, and to grant relief to you who are afflicted as well as to us,* when the Lord Jesus is revealed from heaven with his mighty angels in flaming fire, inflicting vengeance on those who do not know God and on those who do not obey the gospel of our Lord Jesus. They will suffer the punishment of eternal destruction, away from the presence of the Lord and from the glory of his might, when he comes on that day ...

2 THESSALONIANS 1:6-10A, *italics mine*

We cannot deny God's justice without also denying our own desire for justice and retribution. If we choose to believe that such a concept is beneath human dignity, then we should reject all forms of justice and punishment: police, prisons, courts, fines, and school and parental sanctions. Instead, if we are willing to believe that we require sanctions, then we should not criticize God for His use of sanctions—or for His righteous and holy nature.

We need God's wrath. His promise to bring wrath and justice is liberating. We are freed from any compulsion to take justice into our own hands. We are free to love and to forgive:

> Bless those who persecute you; bless and do not curse them. Rejoice with those who rejoice, weep with those who weep. Live in harmony with one another. Do not be haughty, but associate with the lowly. Never be wise in your own sight. Repay no one evil for evil, but give thought to do what is honorable in the sight of all. If possible, so far as it depends on you, live peaceably with all. Beloved, *never avenge yourselves,* but leave it to the wrath of God, for it is written, *"Vengeance is mine, I will repay, says the Lord."*
>
> ROMANS 12:14-19, *italics mine*

Thus, we are enabled to love and to forgive because we have submitted to God all our desires for vengeance. We can rest and be at peace because He manifests His wrath and vengeance—to some extent—through the criminal justice system (Romans 13:1-5).

The prospect of God's wrath should provoke our prayers, evangelism, and acts of love towards the objects of His wrath.

Daniel prayed for Israel because they deserved the wrath of God:

> "O Lord, according to all your righteous acts, let your anger and your wrath turn away from your city Jerusalem, your holy hill, because for our sins, and for the iniquities of our fathers, Jerusalem and your people have become a byword [a curse word] among all who are around us."
>
> DANIEL 9:16

94

We need to regard others through our spiritually-opened eyes, to see their horrid fate and be moved to compassion. I pray that God would give us all such an awareness.

POSTSCRIPT:
Does Love Require Justice and Punishment?

When I interact with progressive Christians, many of them confront me with the following kinds of thoughts and ideas:

> *Many Christians love the thought of people justly getting what they deserve. To say this another way would be that many Christians love the idea of hell. However, Jesus shows us that it would be better to love our enemies, turn the other cheek, and forgive those who trespass against us.*

At the core of this challenge is the question: "Can the biblical teachings on love and non-retaliation include the love of and pursuit of justice?" Here are some ideas to consider on this subject:

We can attend to love more completely because we know that God guarantees justice:

Beloved, never avenge yourselves, but leave it to the wrath of God, for it is written, "Vengeance is mine, I will repay, says the Lord."

ROMANS 12:19

God is a righteous God who loves justice; we too should love what He loves:

"And will not God give justice to his elect, who cry to him day and night? Will he delay long over them? I tell you, he will give justice to them speedily."

LUKE 18:7-8

He has told you, O man, what is good; and what does the Lord require of you but to do justice, and to love kindness, and to walk humbly with your God?

MICAH 6:8

He who justifies the wicked and he who condemns the righteous are both alike an abomination to the LORD.

PROVERBS 17:15

We even know in our own conscience that to exonerate the guilty is wrong.

If we do not show our love by pursuing justice,
then we hate our neighbors.

If we do not bring charges against the arsonist, he will strike again to the detriment of the innocent. Furthermore, our inaction will justifiably bring about public contempt for our faith.

Governing authorities, those who have been
put in place to uphold justice, are God's ministers.

Therefore, we should support them:

Let every person be subject to the governing authorities. For there is no authority except from God, and those that exist have been instituted by God … for he is God's servant for your good. But if you do wrong, be afraid, for he does not bear the sword in vain. For he is the servant of God, an avenger who carries out God's wrath on the wrongdoer.

ROMANS 13:1, 4

Jesus taught on eternal judgment more than anyone.

If He was not ashamed of hell, then
we shouldn't be ashamed of it either:

"Every tree that does not bear good fruit is cut down and thrown into the fire."

MATTHEW 7:19

"And do not fear those who kill the body but cannot kill the soul. Rather fear him who can destroy both soul and body in hell."

MATTHEW 10:28

We deserve punishment when we do wrong:

> We know that the judgment of God rightly falls on those
> who practice such things.
>
> ROMANS 2:2

There must be consequences for wrongful behaviors. For anyone to claim that the wrongdoer *only* deserves rehabilitation is an unbalanced stance. There is a place for both negative and positive reinforcement. The wrongdoer should not be shielded from feelings of shame and guilt as long as there is a means for him to atone for what he has done. Punishment has been endorsed by all societies throughout history and for good reason. To cite just one common-sense example, parents and schoolteachers willingly admit that rehab is not enough—bullies also need to be punished. It seems that only recent "modern" thinking casts aspersions on this kind of wisdom.

God disciplines His children, sometimes severely:

> And have you forgotten the exhortation that addresses
> you as sons? "My son, do not regard lightly the discipline
> of the Lord, nor be weary when reproved by him. For the
> Lord disciplines the one he loves and chastises every son
> whom he receives." It is for discipline that you have to
> endure. God is treating you as sons. For what son is there
> whom his father does not discipline? If you are left without
> discipline, in which all have participated, then you are
> illegitimate children and not sons. Besides this, we have
> had earthly fathers who disciplined us and we respected
> them. Shall we not much more be subject to the Father of
> spirits and live? For they disciplined us for a short time
> as it seemed best to them, but he disciplines us for our
> good, that we may share his holiness. For the moment all
> discipline seems painful rather than pleasant, but later
> it yields the peaceful fruit of righteousness to those who
> have been trained by it.
>
> HEBREWS 12:5–11

No pain, no gain. No discipline, no righteousness.

If we love our children, we will discipline them and explain why they deserve what they have received.

Even the saints in heaven cried out for justice,
and God was approving:

> They cried out with a loud voice, "O Sovereign Lord, holy and true, how long before you will judge and avenge our blood on those who dwell on the earth?" Then they were each given a white robe and told to rest a little longer, until the number of their fellow servants and their brothers should be complete, who were to be killed as they themselves had been.
>
> REVELATION 6:10-11

Although the progressive might deny it, we have a nature like God's. Therefore, we delight in seeing justice accomplished. When we do not see this, we grieve over the injustice. Eventually, when we lose faith in our justice system, cynicism, decay, and vigilantism will fill the void.

There are times when we cannot move on with our lives until our oppressors receive what is just. Is this wrong? This tendency is so prevalent that it is likely that God implanted a love for justice within us. I must admit that—even when I am watching a movie—I cry with joy and relief when the evildoers are brought to justice. And I am not alone. There are many people who cannot bear listening to the evening news. Hearing story after story when justice is not served is too painful for some.

Jesus taught that we will incur severe punishment,
unless we repent:

> "No, I tell you; but unless you repent, you will all likewise perish. Or those eighteen on whom the tower in Siloam fell and killed them: do you think that they were worse offenders than all the others who lived in Jerusalem? No, I tell you; but unless you repent, you will all likewise perish.
>
> LUKE 13:3-5

Our welfare requires that we suffer consequences for our sins.

Common sense alone should inform us that love requires justice. When our institutions withhold justice and police are given stand-down orders, allowing rioters to destroy and bullies to bully, then the innocent are forced to take the law into their own hands. This is a great prescription for destruction and chaos. In love, then, did God ordain a criminal justice system:

> Submit yourselves for the Lord's sake to every human authority: whether to the emperor, as the supreme authority, or to governors, who are sent by him to punish those who do wrong and to commend those who do right.
>
> 1 PETER 2:13-14

In light of these considerations, a well-rounded understanding of biblical love needs to include the many teachings about the justice and righteousness—and the wrath—of God. A faith that refuses to do this cannot please God. Nor will it be validated in our hearts and lives!

CHAPTER 10

Does God's Love for His Enemies Weaken the Charge of "Injustice"?

Is God really love, or has He misrepresented Himself? And, how could He be love if He condemns to eternal torment those who reject Him? As stated in a previous chapter, there are many uncertainties regarding this subject:

- *Is hell self-chosen?*
- *What form(s) does it take?*
- *Who does the punishing?*
- *Are there degrees of punishment?*
- *Will God provide the option of pulling-the-plug for those who suffer?*

However, let's proceed to another issue: "What is the *earthly fate* of those who refuse God and His promise of eternal bliss?" First of all, the Bible teaches that God loves all of His creation. This is good news:

> The LORD is good to all, and his mercy is over all that he has made.
>
> PSALM 145:9

This is true, even though there are many other factors at play. For example, God will also allow us to reap the consequences of our evil deeds. Beyond the realm of each individual man or woman, this is true at the state and national level as well. After all, why should God exempt warring nations from reaping the dire consequences of their conflict?

"Your evil will chastise you, and your apostasy will reprove you. Know and see that it is evil and bitter for you to forsake the LORD your God; the fear of me is not in you," declares the Lord GOD of hosts.

JEREMIAH 2:19

We should fear God and the consequences of our evil. Even though those who reject God are blessed in this life, they will reap the consequences of their own actions (Galatians 6:7). Nevertheless, Jesus taught that His love extends to all humanity. Therefore, we too must love all people as He does:

"But I say to you, Love your enemies and pray for those who persecute you, so that you may be sons of your Father who is in heaven. For he makes his sun rise on the evil and on the good, and sends rain on the just and on the unjust."

MATTHEW 5:44–45

According to Romans 2:4, it is the goodness of God that leads us to repentance. Although vast numbers of people refuse to confess their sins to God, it seems that He still materially blesses His enemies:

Arise, O LORD! Confront him, subdue him! Deliver my soul from the wicked by your sword, from men by your hand, O LORD, from men of the world whose portion is in this life. You fill their womb with treasure; they are satisfied with children, and they leave their abundance to their infants.

PSALM 17:13–14

As hard as it might be for us to believe, the Lord loves those who hate Him. He even allows them to experience certain "benefits" in this life:

"And when you pray, you must not be like the hypocrites. For they love to stand and pray in the synagogues and at the street corners, that they may be seen by others. Truly, I say to you, they have received their reward."

MATTHEW 6:5

The hypocrites of whom Jesus spoke desired the acclaim of men rather than that of God. Therefore, God mercifully allows them to have the very things they desire. So, how can this be construed as unjust?

Seeing the blessings of the unrepentant, many of God's children are tempted to envy them. After all, we believers tend to have a harder lot than others (1 Peter 4:17). The psalmist wrote about his own struggle with jealousy:

> Behold, these are the wicked; always at ease, they increase
> in riches. All in vain have I kept my heart clean and washed
> my hands in innocence.
>
> PSALM 73:12–13

Evidently, the blessings enjoyed by the wicked were quite obvious. The psalmist continued to struggle with jealousy and resentment until God gave him a glimpse of the big picture—the end of the wicked:

> Truly you set them in slippery places; you make them fall
> to ruin. How they are destroyed in a moment, swept away
> utterly by terrors.
>
> PSALM 73:18–19

God loves even those who hate Him. Does God cause, or perhaps allow, His enemies to be "swept away utterly by terrors"? And, does this happen in concert with the choices His enemies make? I think so. Of their own free will, they choose to flee from the Light of God and into the comfort of their own darkness and self-deceit (John 3:19-20).

Can we blame God for this state of affairs? He claims that He wants all to come to salvation (2 Peter 3:9). I feel that I know Him well enough to trust that this is true. Nevertheless, He will not commandeer obedience; He will not force His enemies to obey Him.

~

None of us can possibly understand God entirely, for "The secret things belong to the LORD our God..." (Deuteronomy 29:29a). Perhaps it would not be beneficial for us to know certain things. For instance, if God precisely revealed that aborted and stillborn babies would go to heaven, concerned mothers might be tempted to kill their babies to insure their salvation. I think that this same principle pertains to many other things. For example, can we entirely understand our wives or husbands, or even ourselves? Some things we must simply accept. This is even more true when we are dealing with the Creator of the universe.

Most of humanity does not accept the need for suffering. According to the wisdom of the world, the idea of suffering raises doubts about the love of God. Yet, in so many ways, suffering is necessary. Imagine a world without suffering. In such a world, everything would become meaningless—divorce, immorality, any form of loss or victimization! We would take everything for granted, even the help and the love we receive from others. Without consequences, there would be no lessons, no growth, no compassion, no virtue. There would be no tears of joy or even of sorrow. Perhaps, then, even death would be an expression of God's mercy.

CHAPTER 11

Does God Partner with Evil?

The Bible consistently teaches that there is no evil or unrighteousness in God. Yet there are passages in Scripture where it seems as if God is partnering with evil:

> The coming of the lawless one is by the activity of Satan with all power and false signs and wonders, and with all wicked deception for those who are perishing, because they refused to love the truth and so be saved. Therefore God sends them a strong delusion, so that they may believe what is false, in order that all may be condemned who did not believe the truth but had pleasure in unrighteousness.
>
> 2 THESSALONIANS 2:9-12

Although we can clearly see Satan at his work of deceiving, this passage is also claiming that "God sends them a strong delusion." This suggests that God and the devil are partners in deception. Yet, how do we see God deceiving in these verses? Perhaps by simply allowing Satan and evil to have their ways.

Is it possible that God "send[ing] them a strong delusion" might be understood as God taking away His protection from those who consistently reject Him? For, if God took away His protection, then Satan would be free to deceive those who reject the Lord and His truth. They would be wide open to accepting whatever it is that they prefer—over God.

I think that this is true. In the Book of Romans, Paul refers to those who consistently suppress the truth of God, even though they know Him. Once they reach a certain point, He gives them the liberty to pursue the desires of their hearts:

> Claiming to be wise, they became fools ... Therefore God gave them up in the lusts of their hearts to impurity, to the dishonoring of their bodies among themselves, because they exchanged the truth about God for a lie and worshiped and served the creature rather than the Creator, who is blessed forever! Amen. For this reason God gave them up to dishonorable passions. For their women exchanged natural relations for those that are contrary to nature; and the men likewise gave up natural relations with women and were consumed with passion for one another, men committing shameless acts with men and receiving in themselves the due penalty for their error. And since they did not see fit to acknowledge God, God gave them up to a debased mind to do what ought not to be done.
>
> ROMANS 1:22, 24-28

When God gives up on such people, a vacuum is left which Satan can easily fill. It seems that, ordinarily, the righteous enjoy the umbrella of God's protection. In the first chapter of the Book of Job, Satan complained that Job was righteous only because God had protected him:

> Then Satan answered the LORD and said, "Does Job fear God for no reason? Have you not put a hedge around him and his house and all that he has, on every side?"
>
> JOB 1:9-10A

Satan understandably wanted to afflict Job. God allowed it but also set certain limits. This also seems to have been the case with Peter, who had proudly proclaimed that he would never abandon Jesus:

> "Simon, Simon, behold, Satan demanded to have you, that he might sift you like wheat, but I have prayed for you that your faith may not fail. And when you have turned again, strengthen your brothers."
>
> LUKE 22:31–32

Jesus implied that He would allow Satan to humble Peter, but only temporarily. After Peter did the very thing that he promised he'd never do—deny and disown Jesus—the once-proud fisherman wept tears of repentance. Only after he was humbled was Peter able to do the job for which he had been ordained.

These passages reveal that Jesus doesn't partner with evil but allows evil for His own righteous purposes. He does this by removing His protection, allowing Satan to pursue his destructive agenda.

This principle also seems to pertain to church excommunication for those who, over and over again, refuse to turn away from their sins:

> When you are assembled in the name of the Lord Jesus and my spirit is present, with the power of our Lord Jesus, you are to deliver this man to Satan for the destruction of the flesh, so that his spirit may be saved in the day of the Lord.
>
> 1 CORINTHIANS 5:4-5
> *see also 1 Timothy 1:20*

On the surface, it seems that Paul is asking the church to partner with Satan to bring this unrepentant man to turn from his sin. However, two facts mitigate against such a view. In the first place, Satan has no interest in leading anyone back to God. Secondly, Paul consistently taught against having any contact with the demonic world.

How then are we to understand the phrase: "... to deliver this man to Satan"? It is true that excommunication leaves the unrepentant person vulnerable to Satan. However, while Satan's intent is to do evil, God's intent is to bring the unrepentant back to God. In much the same way, God allowed Job to suffer so that his spiritual arrogance might be revealed, and that Job would come to his senses. And so it is that when a church excommunicates someone, the great hope is that the offender might be restored to a right relationship with God.

From this perspective, God does not partner with evil, but allows evil for His own good purposes. God allowed Joseph's evil brothers to sell him as a slave into Egypt to accomplish His good will. Many years later, after their father Jacob had died, Joseph reassured his repentant brothers:

"As for you, you meant evil against me, but God meant it for good, to bring it about that many people should be kept alive, as they are today. So do not fear; I will provide for you and your little ones." Thus he comforted them and spoke kindly to them.

GENESIS 50:20-21

This demonstrates that God makes use of evil for good. He allows Satan to work evil, once again, for His good purposes. Likewise, God allows those who reject Him to reap the consequences of their choices:

"Because they hated knowledge and did not choose the fear of the Lord, would have none of my counsel and despised all my reproof, therefore they shall eat the fruit of their way, and have their fill of their own devices. For the simple are killed by their turning away, and the complacency of fools destroys them."

PROVERBS 1:29-32

Consequently, God does not need to proactively punish evil. He can merely allow evil itself—or Satan—to do His work for Him. And just how does this happen? It happens through the choices of those who turn away from God. Perhaps this is the ultimate form of justice.

CHAPTER 12

Is the Biblical Hell
a Matter of Eternal Torment?

I don't want to bore anyone. However, this topic is absolutely essential. The teaching of eternal torment (ET) has become for many the biggest obstacle for commitment to the Christian faith. There are several people who claim that they cannot accept the biblical God because of the alleged biblical teaching that hell is a matter of eternal torment. Even committed Christians struggle with this doctrine, sometimes to the point where they wonder about the assurance of their salvation. Therefore, we need to re-examine this important issue. Does the Bible require us to believe in eternal torment?

Eternal Torment in the Old Testament

Is there any biblical evidence for eternal torment in the Old Testament? Actually, we find overwhelming evidence that death is the final destination for the unrepentant:

> You have rebuked the nations; *you have made the wicked perish; you have blotted out their name forever and ever. The enemy came to an end in everlasting ruins;* their cities you rooted out; *the very memory of them has perished.*
> PSALM 9:5-6, *italics mine*

In just a little while, *the wicked will be no more;* though you look carefully at his place, *he will not be there* ... But *the wicked will perish;* the enemies of the Lord are like the glory of the pastures; *they vanish*—like smoke *they vanish away* ... But he passed away, and behold, *he was no more; though I sought him, he could not be found.*

> PSALM 37:10, 20, 36, *italics mine*
> *see also Psalm 68:2 and Hosea 13:2*

Their graves are their homes forever, their dwelling places to all generations, though they called lands by their own names. Man in his pomp will not remain; *he is like the beasts that perish* ... his soul will go to the generation of his fathers, *who will never again see light. Man in his pomp yet without understanding is like the beasts that perish.*

> PSALM 49:11-12, 19-20, *italics mine*

"From new moon to new moon, and from Sabbath to Sabbath, all flesh shall come to worship before me," declares the Lord. "And they shall go out and look on the *dead bodies* of the men who have rebelled against me. *For their worm shall not die* [but their body will die], *their fire shall not be quenched,* and they shall be an abhorrence to all flesh."

> ISAIAH 66:23-24, *italics mine*

"For as you have drunk on my holy mountain, so all the nations shall drink continually; they shall drink and swallow [the cup of God's wrath] *and shall be as though they had never been.*"

> OBADIAH 16:1, *italics mine*

"Behold, when it [the vine] was whole, it was used for nothing. How much less, when the fire has consumed it and it is charred, can it ever be used for anything! Therefore thus says the Lord GOD: *Like the wood of the vine among the trees of the forest, which I have given to the fire for fuel, so have I given up the inhabitants of Jerusalem.*"

> EZEKIEL 15:5–6, *italics mine*

There are many other Old Testament verses which give no indication of ET. To other writers of Scripture, God had revealed the ultimate binary fate of humanity—eternal life, or death. David often demonstrated that he had knowledge of the afterlife. Here is just one example of that knowledge:

> Arise, O Lord! Confront him, subdue him! Deliver my soul from the wicked by your sword, from men by your hand, O Lord, *from men of the world whose portion is in this life.* You fill their womb with treasure; they are satisfied with children, and they leave their abundance to their infants. As for me, *I shall behold your face in righteousness; when I awake, I shall be satisfied with your likeness.*
>
> PSALM 17:13-15, *italics mine*

However, David never indicated any awareness of ET. Asaph was also given a revelation of the fate of humanity following this present life:

> *How they are destroyed in a moment,* swept away utterly by terrors … You guide me with your counsel, and *afterward you will receive me to glory. Whom have I in heaven but you?* And there is nothing on earth that I desire besides you … For behold, *those who are far from you shall perish; you put an end to everyone who is unfaithful to you.*
>
> PSALM 73:19, 24-25, 27, *italics mine*

Although the writers of the Old Testament were not given the fullness of the New Testament revelation, they still had knowledge of heaven and also its corollary—eternal death. ET was entirely unknown to the Old Testament.

Eternal Torment in the New Testament

Jesus' Teachings:

> "Enter by the narrow gate. For the gate is wide and the way is easy that leads to *destruction,* and those who enter by it are many."
>
> MATTHEW 7:13, *italics mine*

"Do not be afraid of those who kill the body but cannot kill the soul. Rather, be afraid of the One who can *destroy both soul and body in hell.*"

MATTHEW 10:28, *italics mine*

"For God so loved the world, that he gave his only Son, that whoever believes in him should not *perish* but have eternal life."

JOHN 3:16, *italics mine*

"Whoever believes in the Son has eternal life, but *whoever rejects the Son will not* [ESV, "never"] *see life,* for God's wrath remains on him."

JOHN 3:36, *italics mine*

"If anyone does not abide in me *he is thrown away like a branch and withers; and the branches are gathered, thrown into the fire, and burned.*"

JOHN 15:6, *italics mine*

"Just as the weeds are gathered and *burned with fire,* so will it be at the end of the age. The Son of Man will send his angels, and they will gather out of his kingdom all causes of sin and all law-breakers and *throw them into the fiery furnace.* In that place there will be weeping and gnashing of teeth."

MATTHEW 13:40–42, *italics mine*
see also Matthew 13:49-50

"I tell you, many will come from east and west and recline at table with Abraham, Isaac, and Jacob in the kingdom of heaven, while *the sons of the kingdom will be thrown into the outer darkness.* In that place there will be weeping and gnashing of teeth."

MATTHEW 8:11–12, *italics mine*

Although there are indications of torment—"weeping and gnashing of teeth"—in these last few verses, there is no evidence that this torment will be eternal or even long-lasting. Instead, *the fire consumes,* just as it does to weeds that are thrown into a fire (Isaiah 66:24).

Other New Testament Teachings:

Though they know God's righteous decree that *those who practice such things deserve to die,* they not only do them but give approval to those who practice them.

ROMANS 1:32, *italics mine*

For all who have sinned without the law will also *perish* without the law, and all who have sinned under the law will be judged by the law.

ROMANS 2:12, *italics mine*

But what fruit were you getting at that time from the things of which you are now ashamed? For the end of those things is *death.* But now that you have been set free from sin and have become slaves of God, the fruit you get leads to sanctification and its end, eternal life. For *the wages of sin is death,* but the free gift of God is eternal life in Christ Jesus our Lord.

ROMANS 6:21–23, *italics mine*

What if God, desiring to show his wrath and to make known his power, has endured with much patience *vessels of wrath prepared for destruction.*

ROMANS 9:22, *italics mine*

Their destiny is destruction, their god is their stomach, and their glory is in their shame. Their mind is on earthly things.

PHILIPPIANS 3:19, *italics mine*

They will be punished with everlasting destruction and shut out from the presence of the Lord and from the majesty of his power.

2 THESSALONIANS 1:9, *italics mine*

For if we go on sinning deliberately after receiving the knowledge of the truth, there no longer remains a sacrifice for sins, but a fearful expectation of judgment, and *a fury of fire that will consume the adversaries.*

HEBREWS 10:26–27, 39, *italics mine*

There is only one lawgiver and judge, *he who is able to save and to destroy.* But who are you to judge your neighbor?

JAMES 4:12, italics mine

But these, like irrational animals, creatures of instinct, *born to be caught and destroyed,* blaspheming about matters of which they are ignorant, will also be *destroyed in their destruction ...*

2 PETER 2:12, italics mine

He who has the Son has life; *he who does not have the Son of God does not have life.*

1 JOHN 5:12, italics mine

... if by turning the cities of *Sodom and Gomorrah to ashes he condemned them to extinction,* making them *an example of what is going to happen to the ungodly.*

2 PETER 2:6, italics mine

And the angels who did not stay within their own position of authority, but left their proper dwelling, *he has kept in eternal chains under gloomy darkness until the judgment of the great day*—just as Sodom and Gomorrah and the surrounding cities, which likewise indulged in sexual immorality and pursued unnatural desire, serve as an example by undergoing *a punishment of eternal fire.*

JUDE 6–7, italics mine

We cannot interpret "eternal fire" as "eternal torment." In 2 Peter 2:6 (above), this fire is equated with "extinction." Sodom and Gomorrah ended in ashes. In Jude 6, the "eternal chains" only last "until the judgment of the great day." Therefore, the "eternal fire" mentioned in Jude 7 cannot be taken in the usual way. The fire, which consumed Sodom, did not last eternally. Instead, it is depicted here as a symbol of the eternal destruction that would occur after the judgment. In Jude 13, we can see that "utter darkness ... reserved forever" is perhaps an indication that the candle of life has been extinguished.

Problem Verses

"And these will go away into eternal punishment [perhaps "eternal death"], but the righteous into eternal life."

MATTHEW 25:46

"And the smoke of their torment will rise for ever and ever. There will be no rest day or night for those who worship the beast and its image, or for anyone who receives the mark of its name."

REVELATION 14:11

NOTE: *it is the smoke which "rises forever," not their* ET

"And the devil, who deceived them, was thrown into the lake of burning sulfur, where the beast and the false prophet had been thrown. They will be tormented day and night for ever and ever."

REVELATION 20:10

And the sea gave up the dead who were in it, Death and Hades gave up the dead who were in them, and they were judged, each one of them, according to what they had done. Then Death and Hades were thrown into the lake of fire. *This is the second death,* the lake of fire.

REVELATION 20:13-14, *italics mine*

see also Revelation 21:8

None of these problem verses indicate eternal torment for any humans—only for the devil, the beast, and the false prophet (Revelation 20:10). However, I suspect that the "second death" in "the lake of fire" will also include this unholy trio. Perhaps the second death will replace the everlasting torment of those three.

Is there any evidence that points to the annihilation of the aforementioned unholy trio? Actually, there are many verses that indicate that our Lord will eventually remove each and every form of evil from His world:

For in him all the fullness of God was pleased to dwell, and through him *to reconcile to himself all things, whether on earth or in heaven,* making peace by the blood of his cross.

COLOSSIANS 1:19–20, *emphasis mine*

… as a plan for the fullness of time, *to unite **all** things in him, things in heaven and things on earth.*

EPHESIANS 1:10, *emphasis mine*

… so that at the name of Jesus every knee should bow, in heaven and on earth and under the earth, and *every **tongue** confess that Jesus Christ is Lord,* to the glory of God the Father.

PHILIPPIANS 2:10–11, *emphasis mine*

For as in Adam all die, so also *in Christ shall **all** be made alive.*

1 CORINTHIANS 15:22, *emphasis mine*

These verses suggest that *all* those who remain after the Lord's final victory (Zechariah 14:16) will be reconciled to our Lord. If this is true, then it suggests that the devil and his allies will also have been destroyed (Ezekiel 28:16) at some point prior to this reconciliation. It is quite clear that these evil enemies of God and humankind will never be reconciled to the God they hate.

The only other alternative for understanding the "all" and "every" verses I quoted above is universalism, the idea that all, including the devil, will be saved. This is unthinkable and would condemn the entire Christian faith as unnecessary and irrelevant.

～

If I have made a good case for the idea of eternal death over eternal torment, it must be admitted: the idea of eternal death is still horrific to contemplate. Furthermore, it is possible that some form of torment might precede the complete annihilation of those who refuse to serve God.

Speaking of those who refuse to serve God, if God is all-merciful, is He required to grant eternal life to those who consistently reject Him (John 3:17-20)? The answer is obvious. Besides, if anyone hates God in this life, he or she will hate Him even more in the life to come. After all, for those who refuse Him now, His exposing light and unassailable purity will be even more intolerable then—in the next life:

> The sinners in Zion are afraid; trembling has seized the godless: "Who among us can dwell with the consuming fire? Who among us can dwell with everlasting burnings?" He who walks righteously and speaks uprightly, who despises the gain of oppressions, who shakes his hands, lest they hold a bribe, who stops his ears from hearing of bloodshed and shuts his eyes from looking on evil.
>
> ISAIAH 33:14–15

Consequently, those who hate God will not repent … they will flee from His presence:

> Then the kings of the earth and the great ones and the generals and the rich and the powerful, and everyone, slave and free, hid themselves in the caves and among the rocks of the mountains, calling to the mountains and rocks, "Fall on us and hide us from the face of him who is seated on the throne, and from the wrath of the Lamb, for the great day of their wrath has come, and who can stand?"
>
> REVELATION 6:15-17
> *see also Isaiah 2:20–21; Psalm 1:5; and Malachi 3:2*

It seems that if those who refuse to serve God want the rocks to fall on them, then they would surely prefer non-existence rather than an existence with God. Shouldn't the Lord allow them to have what they have chosen for themselves? What could be more just?

CHAPTER 13

Is Biblical Slavery Unjust?

Those who want to denigrate the Bible often argue that its morality is substandard. Just recently, one young man angrily charged that the institution of biblical slavery was all that he needed to reject the Bible. However, I wondered whether he had really taken the time to try to understand this practice.

First of all, biblical slavery was never conceived or practiced in a racial way, as it had been in the United States and in other nations. Actually, biblical slavery—or servanthood—was quite humane compared to what it was like being incarcerated in prison.

Kidnapping in order to enslave was strictly forbidden in the Old Testament.

> "Anyone who kidnaps another and either sells him or still has him when he is caught must be put to death."
>
> EXODUS 21:16

The New Testament, in 1 Timothy 1:10, also forbids kidnapping for the purpose of slavery. Instead, biblical slavery was instituted to address the problem of unpaid debts and criminality:

> "A thief must certainly make restitution, but if he has nothing, he must be sold to pay for his theft."
>
> EXODUS 22:3

This practice was regarded as just; in fact, it was far more just than simple imprisonment or having your hand cut off. Although it must be admitted that slavery was degrading, the biblical version of it was also humane:

> "If a fellow Hebrew, a man or a woman, sells himself to you and serves you six years, in the seventh year you must let him go free. And when you release him, do not send him away empty-handed. Supply him liberally from your flock, your threshing floor and your winepress. Give to him as the Lord your God has blessed you."
>
> DEUTERONOMY 15:12-14

In many instances, an Israelite slave could be redeemed by their family members (Leviticus 25:48). Even if the family of a slave wouldn't or couldn't redeem him, the slave was to be released after six years of labor.

The institution of biblical slavery also provided legal protections for the slave.

> "If a man hits a manservant or maidservant in the eye and destroys it, he must let the servant [or "slave"] go free to compensate for the eye. And if he knocks out the tooth of a manservant or maidservant, he must let the servant go free to compensate for the tooth."
>
> EXODUS 21:26-27

The slave or servant was to be treated almost like family.

Slaves were to travel with their "families" to Jerusalem and to rejoice as they ate their offerings—together, with the family. Servants/slaves were considered part of the household:

> "And there [at the Temple] you shall eat before the LORD your God, and you shall rejoice, *you and your households,* in all that you undertake, in which the LORD your God has blessed you ... then to the place that the LORD your God will choose, to make his name dwell there, there you shall bring all that I command you: your burnt offerings and your sacrifices, your tithes and the contribution that

you present, and all your finest vow offerings that you vow to the LORD. And you shall rejoice before the LORD your God, *you and your sons and your daughters, your male servants and your female servants,* and the Levite that is within your towns, since he has no portion or inheritance with you."

> DEUTERONOMY 12:7, 11-12, *italics mine*
> see also *Deuteronomy 16:11-15 and 26:11*

Slavery also addressed the problem of what to do with a defeated enemy.

While ancient practice entailed the extermination of males and the sexual abuse of females, the Bible prohibited this:

"When you go to war against your enemies and the Lord your God delivers them into your hands and you take captives, if you notice among the captives a beautiful woman and are attracted to her, you may take her as your wife … If you are not pleased with her, let her go wherever she wishes. You must not sell her or treat her as a slave, since you have dishonored her."

> DEUTERONOMY 21:10-11, 14

Biblical slavery did not allow the dividing of families.

Although the dividing of families was practiced under the auspices of racial slavery, it was not allowed according to biblical slavery:

When you buy a Hebrew slave, he shall serve six years, and in the seventh he shall go out free, for nothing. If he comes in single, he shall go out single; if he comes in married, then his wife shall go out with him.

> EXODUS 21:2-3

When a secularist sees such a verse, he or she might protest: "Well, this only applies to the Hebrew slave." Although this is true, any slave could choose to become an Israelite; then, that slave would be given the same rights as any Hebrew slave.

Mosaic Law was inclusive. God commanded Abraham that even those he bought as slaves were to be circumcised, thereby erasing any possible class or racial distinction within his "household":

> "This is my covenant with you [Abraham] and your descendants after you, the covenant you are to keep: Every male among you shall be circumcised. You are to undergo circumcision, and it will be the sign of the covenant between me and you. For the generations to come every male among you who is eight days old must be circumcised, including those born in your household or bought with money from a foreigner—those who are not your offspring."
>
> GENESIS 17:10-12

Israel was to be a model of inclusiveness. All could come to God; all were to be under the covenant of God and none were ever turned away:

> "Any slave you have bought may eat of it [the Passover] after you have circumcised him … An alien living among you who wants to celebrate the LORD'S Passover must have all the males in his household circumcised; then he may take part like one born in the land. No uncircumcised male may eat of it. The same law applies to the native-born and to the alien living among you."
>
> EXODUS 12:44, 48-49

Once again, even the slave could choose circumcision and receive full inclusion as an Israelite. It had been God's intention that Israel would be the model of inclusion, and circumcision was the ticket into the "family." Race, education, national origin—none of these would be an obstacle. God intended that everyone would be under the same law.

Furthermore, there was never any indication of racial superiority in any of Israel's legislation. Instead, Israel was always reminded that they had once been slaves and thus, they were to be gracious to their slaves. A single egalitarian set of laws would be the rule for all—whether Jewish or not. Israel was to be a model society for all the surrounding nations:

"See, I [Moses] have taught you decrees and laws as the LORD my God commanded me, so that you may follow them in the land you are entering to take possession of it. Observe them carefully, for this will show your wisdom and understanding to the nations, who will hear about all these decrees and say, 'Surely this great nation is a wise and understanding people.' What other nation is so great as to have their gods near them the way the LORD our God is near us whenever we pray to him? And what other nation is so great as to have such righteous decrees and laws as this body of laws I am setting before you today?"

DEUTERONOMY 4:5-8

∿

Predictably, secularism now wants to claim the mantle of "the protector of human rights." This certainly wasn't the case under secular communism; nor has it been the case historically. "Secularism does not liberate," according to Indian scholar Vishal Mangalwadi. He quotes historian Rodney Stark to support his claim:

A virtual Who's Who of "Enlightenment" figures fully accepted slavery ... It was not philosophers or secular intellectuals who assembled the moral indictment of slavery, but the very people they held in such contempt: men and women having intense Christian faith, who opposed slavery because it was sin ... The larger point is that abolitionists, whether popes or evangelists, spoke almost exclusively in the language of Christian faith ... Although many Southern clergy [in America] proposed theological defenses of slavery, pro-slavery rhetoric was overwhelmingly secular—references were made to "liberty" and "states' rights," not to "sin" or "salvation." [1]

Biblical slavery differs from other forms of slavery as the punishment of the innocent differs from the punishment of the guilty. Dinesh D'Souza adds:

Christians were the first group in history to start an anti-slavery movement. The movement started in late eighteenth century in Britain...In England, William Wilberforce spear-headed a campaign that began with almost no support and was driven entirely by his Christian convictions...Pressed by religious groups at home, England took the lead in repressing the slave trade abroad.[2]

The Second Great Awakening, which started in the early 19th century and coursed through New England and New York and then through the interior of the country, left in its wake the temperance movement, the movement of women's suffrage, and most important, the abolitionist movement.[3]

The secularist charges that the New Testament condones even non-biblical slavery. This is not true. However, the New Testament does counsel the Christian slave to be faithful to his "master," as he should be to any employer or even prison guard. This is because we are commanded to show love and kindness to *all*, even to those who have treated us badly.

Hopefully, it is becoming apparent that much of the criticism against the righteousness of God is without merit.

CHAPTER 14

Do God's "Offensive" Judgments Make Him Unjust?

One atheist woman wrote that a God who would drown the human race in a worldwide flood—including children—wasn't worthy of worship. Others invoke God's destruction of the Canaanites to make the same point.

Do these judgments prove that God is unjust? But first, who is to say what is just or unjust? Our conscience? However, if our conscience is no more than a set of biochemical reactions, then why should our conscience have the authority to dictate moral judgments? After all, the biochemical reactions involved are merely physical phenomena, not moral dictates. The judgments of our conscience should be no more determinative than the judgments of a thermometer—that is, if hot and cold do not objectively exist. Instead, a thermometer has relevance only if hot and cold do exist. In the same way, our conscience has relevance *only if God and His moral code exist.*

Thus, we can understand why it is that some choose to deny that our conscience is calibrated to discern right and wrong, or what is just or unjust:

- Only the existence of a righteous God could provide such a rationale.
- However, the existence of this God would also mean that we are no longer autonomous—instead, we would be liable to His judgments.

- This worldview or perspective would then also mean that the guilt and shame we experience could not be dismissed as simply a biochemical reaction. It would be evidence of the reality of God's displeasure and of our need to reconcile with Him.

- Such a paradigm would mean that our conscience would warn us about living the life *we want to live*. Instead, it would guide us to live the life that *we should be living*.

However, if objective moral truths and laws do not exist, then we are forced to make up moral judgments according to what works for us—pragmatism—and what gives us benefits.

To deny the existence of a righteous God gives us leverage to say "no" to our troubling conscience. But to deny our conscience is to deny a part of ourselves, including socially-needful boundaries like objective human rights. Without such rights, could anyone coherently say, "You have no right to touch me," if human rights are just a concept that we created? That would be like playing chess without rules, a meaningless and unfulfilling endeavor.

Consequently, when it suits us, we invoke our moral intuition to claim, "I know right from wrong. I don't need God to be good." But then, on other occasions, we turn off any semblance of a moral code and claim, "You have no right to judge me. What you are saying is just true for you."

Let's apply this now to our judgments against the righteousness of God. We can logically say that the righteous standards of the God of the Bible offend us. We can also say that we are troubled by His destruction of the Canaanites, the cities of Sodom and Gomorrah, and the whole world, destroying almost all of mankind in the flood. However, we cannot logically say that God is unjust if we lack an objective standard of justice. Likewise, we cannot logically say that God is unjust if "justice" is just a concept we made up. For such judgments to carry any moral authority, we must assume that there are moral laws that are above us and more authoritative than our own thoughts and preferences. This requires God!

If the law of justice has a real existence, as does the law of gravity, there must be a Law-Giver—One whose opinions and edicts are far greater than our own. This is the Creator Himself. Therefore, we cannot use the dictates of our conscience to deny the existence of the One who wrote these objective laws into our conscience in the first place. Without Him, we cannot have laws. All we would have would be biochemical reactions which happen to feel like laws. As offensive as the worldwide flood and its destruction seems to us, we cannot logically raise an objection against it—that is, if it is only a matter of our own sentiments. There must be an eminently authoritative Being standing behind such far-reaching judgments.

As offensive as this line of reasoning might seem to some, it is unassailable. Without the Law-Giver, there cannot be any authoritative moral laws at all, just changing fads and fancies.

Without objective moral laws, this vacuum can be filled only by brute, coercive human power. How else can we resist the logic of a serial killer like Ted Bundy, who confessed to over 30 gruesome murders?

> Then I learned that all moral judgments are 'value judgments,' that all value judgments are subjective, and that none can be proved to be either 'right' or 'wrong' ... I discovered that to become truly free, truly unfettered, I had to become truly uninhibited. And I quickly discovered that the greatest obstacle to my freedom, the greatest block and limitation to it, consists in the insupportable "value judgments" that I was bound to respect the rights of others. I asked myself, who were these 'others?' Other human beings with human rights? Why is it more wrong to kill a human animal than any other animal, a pig or a sheep or a steer? Is your life more to you than a hog's life to a hog? ... In any case, let me assure you, my dear young lady, that there is absolutely no comparison between the pleasure I might take in eating ham and the pleasure I anticipate in raping and murdering you.[1]

∿

If God is the Source of all our moral laws, doesn't He have the right and even duty to enforce these laws and to bring justice? If the world, the Canaanites, and Sodom and Gomorrah repeatedly violated His laws—laws which He had also implanted into our conscience—why should He not have the right to bring justice? This is His world, and we are His creation.

However, we can always pose questions like:

- *Couldn't God have made the world better?*
- *If He is all-powerful, why couldn't He have made creatures who would not suffer so much and then die?*
- *Couldn't He have stopped Hitler and Stalin from their genocidal rampages?*

There are endless questions just like these, but they all overlook the possibility that God might have good reasons for what He does and what He allows. Is it reasonable for us to reject God because there are unanswered questions? Do we reject science, even though it does not adequately answer even the most basic questions—what is light, matter, time, or space?

Is it possible that God will compensate our momentary suffering here—in the vastness of eternity? Perhaps, but we don't know. Perhaps God has purposes that lie beyond our comprehension. However, it would be wise for us not to reject Him because of the things that transcend our understanding. Instead, we should accept and adore God because of the many other things that we do understand about Him!

Once again, many have called God a "baby killer" because the worldwide flood washed away the children along with all the evil people. However, should God be under obligation to intervene on behalf of the children of evil parents? Should those who are wicked be given God's assurance that their children will never have to pay the price for their evil?

I believe that God has His reasons. I worked for the New York City Department of Probation for 15 years. Occasionally, a probationer would confess, "Mr. Mann, I am now a father. I need to get my life together for the sake of my child." He understood that his child was his responsibility, and that he shouldn't count on God to make up for his failures. But what if he had the assurance that God would care for his child even if he returned to criminality? It would be like receiving a monthly welfare check, relieving him of any of his responsibilities, and to the detriment of his entire family.

There were many things about God that His most illustrious theologian, Paul, failed to understand:

Oh, the depth of the riches and wisdom and knowledge of God! How unsearchable are his judgments and how inscrutable his ways! "For who has known the mind of the Lord, or who has been his counselor?" "Or who has given a gift to him that he might be repaid?" For from him and through him and to him are all things. To him be glory forever. Amen.

ROMANS 11:33-36

Despite his limited understanding, Paul proceeded in confidence. True, there are things about God that are troubling. But we must recognize that we are severely limited in what we can understand, and thus we should be especially careful not to judge Him. In fact, we must accept the truth that the Creator has a right and even a duty to judge His creation.

~

All the Prophets of Israel had their problems with God, whom they often failed to understand. For example, the Prophet Elijah had complained:

"O LORD my God, have you brought calamity even upon the widow with whom I sojourn, by killing her son?"

1 KINGS 17:20

The Prophet Jonah wanted no part of preaching to Nineveh, a people which had caused such great suffering to Israel. After God had forgiven Nineveh, Jonah was angry with God:

"Therefore now, O LORD, please take my life from me, for it is better for me to die than to live." And the LORD said, "Do you do well to be angry?"

JONAH 4:3-4

God had directed the Prophet Jeremiah:

"Go up and down the streets of Jerusalem, look around and consider, search through her squares. If you can find but one person who deals honestly and seeks the truth, I will forgive this city."

JEREMIAH 5:1-2

However, Jeremiah was convinced that God's assessment of Israel was way off:

> I thought, "These are only the poor; they are foolish, for they do not know the way of the LORD, the requirements of their God. So I will go to the leaders and speak to them; surely they know the way of the LORD, the requirements of their God."
>
> JEREMIAH 5:4-5

Each of these prophets was convinced that God had been mistaken. Jeremiah later discovered that God's assessment had been spot-on, especially after he discovered that even his own, educated, priestly family had wanted to kill him.

The Prophet Habakkuk had asked God to intervene. His nation of Judah had become utterly corrupt and sinful. However, after God had revealed to Habakkuk His extreme solution—bringing the Babylonians against Judah—the prophet balked:

> You are of purer eyes than to behold evil, and cannot look on wickedness. Why do You look on those who deal treacherously, and hold Your tongue when the wicked [Babylonia] devours a person [Jerusalem] more righteous than he?
>
> HABAKKUK 1:13

Habakkuk was unable to understand as God understood until he received further revelation from Him.

The Prophet Isaiah felt that God was being too strict with Israel. He even accused God of withholding His mercy, since God was the Potter and Israel the clay. Consequently, the Potter could mold the clay into a perfect vessel:

> Yet, O LORD, you are our Father. We are the clay, you are the potter; we are all the work of your hand. Do not be angry beyond measure, O LORD; do not remember our sins forever. Oh, look upon us, we pray, for we are all your people ... After all this, O LORD, will you hold yourself back? Will you keep silent and punish us beyond measure?
>
> ISAIAH 64:8-9,12

Isaiah understood that God the Potter *could* change the heart of the sinful Israelites. But this is something that He would not do, at least, not at that time. Isaiah also complained that God's punishment was too extreme.

The examples we have seen from studying these prophets illustrate an important point: None of us understand God comprehensively. Our vision is quite narrow.

This reminds me of a visit to the Museum of Natural History in New York City where we viewed a display on waves. Although there are many forms of waves, we can see only a very small range of them. Similarly, when we glance down at our wristwatch, we can see the second-hand move. However, it is doubtful that we can see the minute-hand move; and we cannot see the hour-hand move. Our vision and our understanding are very limited.

If we apply this principle to the Creator—who is even greater than His creation—we must conclude:

> "For my thoughts are not your thoughts, neither are your ways my ways," declares the LORD. "For as the heavens are higher than the earth, so are my ways higher than your ways and my thoughts than your thoughts."
>
> ISAIAH 55:8–9

Should we be satisfied with the little that God has revealed about Himself and His ways? For me, the answer is a resounding *yes*. Why? He has proved Himself to me in many ways. I also know how limited my understanding is and how additional divine revelation might simply confuse me. Although I continually seek further understanding, I am aware that I am in no position to bring accusations against my Creator. Accurate judgment requires exhaustive understanding of what is and what might have been if God had planned things differently.

Yet, it is no surprise that I—and many others like me—continue to be tempted to bring forth accusations against God. I suppose one could say that we are in good company—the prophets of old did the same thing.

CHAPTER 15

Is God an "Egomaniac"?

While our God could be misconstrued as an egomaniac, this charge represents a misunderstanding of His loving intentions. Here is a verse of Scripture that is cited by those who wish to denigrate God:

> But when Jesus heard [of the cry for Jesus to come and heal Lazarus], he said, "This illness does not lead to death. It is *for the glory of God, so that the Son of God may be glorified* through it."
>
> JOHN 11:4, *italics mine*

Here is how one of the critics might reason: "See how Jesus used the eventual death of Lazarus for his own selfish purpose, to glorify Himself? Who could believe in such a self-centered God?"

Was seeking God's glory a matter of being self-centered? It does not appear to be so. Instead, Jesus' glory had been manifested to build the faith of His disciples:

> Then Jesus told them plainly, "Lazarus has died, and *for your sake* I am glad that I was not there, *so that you may believe*. But let us go to him."
>
> JOHN 11:14–15, *italics mine*

How would the disciples believe? By beholding the glory of God through the resurrection of Lazarus, who had been in the grave for four days. In view of this, the disciples beholding Jesus' glory in the raising of Lazarus was a manifestation of the love of God. It reassured them that the Savior was truly able to take care of them—and us:

> Jesus said, "Take away the stone." Martha, the sister of the dead man, said to him, "Lord, by this time there will be an odor, for he has been dead four days." Jesus said to her, "Did I not tell you that if you believed *you would see the glory of God?*" So they took away the stone. And Jesus lifted up his eyes and said, "Father, I thank you that you have heard me. I knew that you always hear me, but I said this on account of the people standing around, *that they may believe that you sent me.*"
>
> JOHN 11:39–42, *italics mine*

Our faith requires its daily bread and nourishment, the reassurance that Jesus is who He claimed to be. Besides building up the faith of His disciples, many others came to faith through this display of His glory. In fact, Jesus prayed to the Father that we—even today—might behold His glory:

> "I do not ask for these only, but also for those who will believe in me through their word ... Father, I desire that they also, whom you have given me, may be with me where I am, *to see my glory* that you have given me because you loved me before the foundation of the world. O righteous Father, even though the world does not know you, I know you, and these know that you have sent me. I made known to them your name [character], and I will continue to make it known, *that the love with which you have loved me may be in them,* and I in them."
>
> JOHN 17:20, 24–26, *italics mine*

Why did Jesus pray for us to see His glory? So that the love of God would also be in us! This is hardly the heart of an egomaniac. I therefore rejoice in the glory of God. And, since Jesus gave His glory to us, according to John 17:22, it is also our glory.

CHAPTER 16

Does God's Omnipotence Make Him Unjust?

Writing for *The New York Times*, professor of philosophy, Peter Atterton, claimed that the biblical revelation of God doesn't make logical sense:

> As a philosopher myself, I'd like to focus on a specific question: Does the idea of a morally perfect, all-powerful, all-knowing God make sense? Does it hold together when we examine it logically?[1]

Atterton first examines the attribute of God's omnipotence:

> You've probably heard the paradox of the stone before: Can God create a stone that cannot be lifted? If God can create such a stone, then He is not all powerful, since He Himself cannot lift it. On the other hand, if He cannot create a stone that cannot be lifted, then He is not all powerful, since He cannot create the unliftable stone. Either way, God is not all powerful.[2]

In other words, *God is not all-powerful* because He cannot do the illogical, like making a stone which is both liftable and unliftable. Nor can He exist and not exist at the same time.

This points to the fact that Atterton fails to understand the biblical revelation of God's omnipotence. While God can do everything He wants to do, He can't do it in any manner. He cannot sin and He cannot violate His nature. Furthermore, it seems as if being logical might even be part of His un-violable nature. In other words, perhaps God cannot be illogical.

Even if the example of the liftable/unliftable rock fails to prove his point, Atterton has another stone to throw:

> ... can God create a world in which evil does not exist? This does appear to be logically possible. Presumably God could have created such a world without contradiction. It evidently would be a world very different from the one we currently inhabit, but a possible world all the same. Indeed, if God is morally perfect, it is difficult to see why he wouldn't have created such a world. So why didn't He?[3]

He did create such a world, but *we* screwed it up. The result was the Fall. Yes, God could have created us without the freewill to do evil, but perhaps He had a good reason for not making us robotic.

In his defense, Atterton quotes Charles Darwin:

> "... for what advantage can there be in the sufferings of millions of the lower animals throughout almost endless time?"[4]

According to Atterton and Darwin, a good and omnipotent Being would not have allowed our sinful choices to bring suffering upon the animal kingdom—or even upon our own children. In other words, they have claimed that, "I don't see the point in this; therefore, any good and omnipotent God wouldn't have done things this way."

Job had also believed that God couldn't possibly be just and righteous, since He had caused or allowed Job so suffer. Job actually accused God of being unjust. He had been convinced that he understood enough about God to bring such a charge against Him. However, at the end of the *Book of Job*, in chapters 38-41, God asked Job a series of questions, none of which he could answer. Job got the point: If he couldn't even answer the basics, how could he impugn God's justice? Therefore, Job repented in dust and ashes.

Job had demanded his "day in court," and he got it—to his great chagrin.

Atterton attempts one last, desperate "Hail-Mary":

> A morally perfect being would never get enjoyment from causing pain to others. Therefore, God doesn't know what it is like to be human. In that case He doesn't know what we know. But if God doesn't know what we know, God is not all knowing, and the concept of God is contradictory. God cannot be both omniscient and morally perfect. Hence, God could not exist.[5]

Atterton's charge that God gets "enjoyment from causing pain to others" is unfounded. How could he know what God experiences? Did God confide in him? This brings us back again to Atterton's faulty logic:

> If I cannot make any sense out of it, it means that there is no sense in it.[6]

However, the Bible indicates that God allows and even redirects evil to accomplish His good purposes. We might not see those purposes in what He does and what He allows, but this does not mean that He does not have good reasons for what He allows to happen. The Bible assures us that He does:

> ... we rejoice in our sufferings, knowing that suffering produces endurance, and endurance produces character, and character produces hope, and hope does not put us to shame, because God's love has been poured into our hearts through the Holy Spirit who has been given to us.
>
> ROMANS 5:3–5

God is teaching us priceless lessons through what we suffer. However, it doesn't seem that Atterton is willing to consider this possibility. Perhaps we think too much of our ability to understand. Is it possible that the attainment of a couple of PhDs might have inflated Atterton's estimation of what he could understand?

Nevertheless, even with all the education we might receive, we miss a lot. For example, we can see only a very small range of light or hear an equally small range of audio vibrations. We cannot see what birds see or hear what dogs hear. We cannot navigate as the Monarch butterfly can, all the way from the northern United States to its winter haven deep in Mexico. We are limited creatures who must find our fulfillment in the bosom of our Creator and Redeemer. He is our home, our resting place—and our trust must be in Him!

~

Other skeptics claim:

> *If God is all-powerful and all-benevolent, there shouldn't be suffering. It is completely unnecessary. He should have been able to do a better job.*

I admit that we cannot *completely* explain why God causes or allows suffering. Yet, it is clear to me that I need to suffer for God to accomplish His purposes in my life:

> [We are] persecuted, but not forsaken; struck down, but not destroyed; always carrying in the body the death of Jesus, so that the life of Jesus may also be manifested in our bodies. For we who live are always being given over to death for Jesus' sake, so that the life of Jesus also may be manifested in our mortal flesh.
>
> 2 CORINTHIANS 4:9–11

Without suffering, I would never have learned compassion, humility, or forgiveness. Through suffering, He has taught me to forgive and to appreciate others, even more than myself.

The skeptic cannot rationally claim that suffering is "completely unnecessary." To make such a judgment requires an exhaustive amount of knowledge to explore every possibility. The effects of one action that causes suffering can extend around the world and into millennia, even eternity. While we can question why God allows suffering, to claim that He is, therefore, a monster, transcends our knowledge and our morally relative standards of judgment. Thus, from our very limited perspective, we cannot confidently say that suffering is "completely unnecessary."

This principle also pertains to many other charges. For example: "Your omnipotent god could have done things in a better way." In the *Conclusion*, I will deal more thoroughly with this charge.

Lastly, we shouldn't be surprised that the skeptic can and will find fault with anything that pertains to God's creation. For the skeptical evolutionist, nothing is perfect. He has a vested interest in seeing imperfection—a lack of design—in everything. His naturalistic lens forces him to see imperfection, even where the evidence is not on his side. Consequently, the evolutionist has mistakenly insisted that we are filled with useless and leftover DNA, structures, and organs from "our primate ancestors," only to later be proved wrong.

Nevertheless, I must admit that I am honeycombed with imperfections and age-related defects—my failing eyes, ears, teeth, and back, among other things. However, we Christians accept that this life is just a temporary way station on our arduous journey to our heavenly perfection. We also accept the rationale of the Fall and the resulting brokenness of this world. Yet, we still find overwhelming evidence of the brilliant designs of our Lord.

CHAPTER 17

How Are We to View
the Wrath of God?

Today, it is common to hear people say:

> God is unadulterated love. God is too glorious to hate
> anything or punish anyone. When religious people claim that
> God hates and punishes, it is because they have created a god
> in their own likeness. Instead, God is above all such pettiness.

Commensurate with such thinking, Western society denies that the criminal is accountable, guilty, or deserving of punishment. Here are some of the reasons that might be offered for this position:

1. We—all of humanity—are merely the product of our nurture and nature.

2. We lack freewill and therefore, as far as "criminal" behavior is concerned, we could not have acted otherwise.

3. If a wrongdoer had simply been loved enough, he or she would not have committed a crime. Consequently, the fault lies with the parents and society.

4. We are more likely to regard ourselves as compassionate, "good and worthy people," when we don't seek justice or any punishment for the wrongdoer.

5. Furthermore, we may be more engaged in wrongdoing than previous generations, especially sexually and relationally. We no longer experience any sort of righteous indignation at the sight of the wrongdoing of others.

Moral relativism, the denial of moral absolutes, has become the reigning religion of the West. This has deprived our justice systems of a firm moral foundation upon which to render judgments. Although judgments are still being rendered, they are more based on tradition and expedience than conviction.

In accordance with these beliefs, if a god does exist, this god would be unrighteous if it were wrathful and punitive. Of course, such a god would not be the God of the Bible. There are numerous verses from the Scriptures that claim that *God hates sin*, and that *His wrath is against the unrepentant*. For example:

> If you spurn my statutes, and if your soul abhors my rules, so that you will not do all my commandments, but break my covenant, then I will do this to you: I will visit you with panic, with wasting disease and fever that consume the eyes and make the heart ache. And you shall sow your seed in vain, for your enemies shall eat it. I will set my face against you, and you shall be struck down before your enemies. Those who hate you shall rule over you, and you shall flee when none pursues you.
>
> LEVITICUS 26:15–17

You might not like this God, but you should also consider the alternative—a god who isn't troubled by evil or our inhumanity to our fellow man.

~

God does indeed punish, but it seems as if He is often simply allowing us to reap what we have sown. In other words, He allows us to pursue our own course:

> The backslider in heart will be filled with the fruit of his ways, and a good man will be filled with the fruit of his ways.
>
> PROVERBS 14:14

We will reap what we sow, and our conscience bears witness to this truth. However, in the West, almost no one listens to the wisdom of the

Scriptures. As one acquaintance of mine commented, "We have grown beyond that." So, instead of citing Bible verses, let me try to reason this out with you:

1. If God doesn't punish, then why should we punish? Instead, we should open the prisons. We should allow our children and students to learn without discipline, without any consequences which might be painful. Years ago, when I was subbing at a high school, I was dismissed. Why? I had the audacity to say the following to an administrator, while I was in front of a class: "I have had more disciplinary problems with this class than any of the others." I was informed that it was wrong for me to have said this while in front of the class. Interestingly, the administrator had no problem at all with punishing me—in front of the class!

2. If God doesn't hate rape, why should we hate rape and bother to intervene, especially if there is no objective right or wrong?

3. Indulgence is wrongly associated with love. However, love—the concern for the other person's welfare—might require that we warn or even censure. One of my Bible students confessed that she had consistently indulged her gay friends, even going with them to the clubs. However, looking back, she now regrets that she didn't openly oppose their lifestyle along with its dangers. Instead, she stood by and watched many of her friends die of STDs.

4. Love and the administration of justice are inseparable. To love is to pursue justice; and to pursue justice is to love our neighbor. To not hate rape, bullying, and kidnapping is to not love. To be permissive of injustice is to hate our neighbor. Therefore, the Lord ordained the justice system (Romans 13:1-4).

5. We destroy our youth by teaching them that they are not accountable, that they will not suffer because of their misdeeds. Once again, the law of reaping what one sows should be obvious. Instead, when young people are "raised" by their lawless peer group, they too become lawless.

6. We also destroy society with such errant teachings. According to historians Will and Ariel Durant, this reorientation might pose a real threat to our civilization:

> Caught in the relaxing interval between one moral
> code and the next, an unmoored generation
> surrenders itself to luxury, corruption, and restless
> disorder of family and morals ... At the end of the
> process a decisive defeat in war may bring a final
> blow, or barbarian invasion from without may
> combine with barbarism welling up from within to
> bring the civilization to a close.[1]

Since the sixties in the West, our pleasure-seeking thinking has been accompanied by tremendous growth in the incidence of crime. In addition, there is an increased resistance to the hatred of evil. Economic stagnation is on the upswing.

It is important for us to remember that the success of the West has been predicated on biblical values. Can any people thrive once it abandons these values? However, the arrogance of this age refuses to humble itself before the lessons of history. It believes that it is living in a new age where the old lessons no longer pertain. Yet, history has made it abundantly clear that when a society forfeits justice, its people feel compelled to take justice into their own hands—not a desirable prospect.

The wrath of God—along with the assurance of His love and forgiveness— is absolutely essential for our thriving. In fact, the wrath of God is the very thing that is lacking, in view of the steady decline of the previously Christian West. According to the Scriptures, the fear of God can be a delight. It had been so for the Messiah, Jesus:

> There shall come forth a shoot from the stump of Jesse,
> and a branch from his roots shall bear fruit. And the Spirit
> of the LORD shall rest upon him, the Spirit of wisdom and
> understanding, the Spirit of counsel and might, the Spirit
> of knowledge and the fear of the LORD. And his delight
> shall be in the fear of the LORD. He shall not judge by
> what his eyes see, or decide disputes by what his ears hear,
> but with righteousness he shall judge the poor, and decide
> with equity for the meek of the earth; and he shall strike
> the earth with the rod of his mouth, and with the breath of
> his lips he shall kill the wicked.

> ISAIAH 11:1–4
> *see also John 4:34*

Instead, it seems that sexual license and other forms of self-indulgence are the norm. These are the very things that are dividing and tearing us and our families apart.

I deeply appreciate that, the more we study the wrath of God, the more we can rest assured. This same God guarantees that *He* will bring justice. This frees us up to love—and to leave revenge to Him. Not a bad arrangement at all!

CHAPTER 18

Are God's Judgments
an Embarrassment to Us?

God's Church needs God's disciplines.

I had been troubled by the account of Ananias and Sapphira found in the *Book of Acts*. Like many of the brethren, they had sold some property and had given the proceeds to the apostles for the blessing of the Church. However, even though the couple had only given half of the money from the sale—no sin in itself—they lied and said that they had given over all of the money. Peter's response was absolutely chilling:

> "Ananias, why hath Satan filled thy heart to lie to the Holy Spirit, and to keep back part of the price of the land? While it remained, did it not remain thine own? And after it was sold, was it not in thy power? How is it that thou hast conceived this thing in thy heart? Thou has not lied unto men, but unto God." And Ananias hearing these words fell down and gave up the ghost: and great fear came upon all that heard it.
>
> ACTS 5:3-5 KJV

I was troubled by this. Such a harsh judgment from God and absolutely no expression of remorse from Peter! After all, Ananias did donate half of the proceeds of the money he received. Besides, this was just a little white lie, right?

Then there was the matter of the way in which the apostle had spoken to Ananias' wife. Peter's treatment of Sapphira seemed callous to me, especially in view of her great loss:

> "Tell me whether ye sold the land for so much." And she said, "Yea, for so much." But Peter said unto her, "How is it that ye have agreed together to try the Spirit of the Lord? Behold, the feet of them that have buried thy husband are at the door, and they shall carry thee out." And she fell down immediately at his feet, and gave up the ghost.
>
> ACTS 5:8-10

It seemed as if Peter had given only the briefest opportunity for repentance before pronouncing judgment on this unfortunate woman.

However, after these dramatic judgments, both of which ended with death, here is the record of Scripture:

> And great fear came upon the whole church, and upon all that heard these things.
>
> ACTS 5:11

Well, no wonder! No one is above sin. If such a thing could happen to Ananias and Sapphira, perhaps it could happen to anyone! Who then could serve such a wrathful God? Who could continue to rejoice in Him and regard Him as their Savior, knowing that He might snuff them out at any moment? It seems that some did indeed distance themselves from the early Church because of this, according to Acts 5:13. And who could blame them?

Who could blame us, as members of Western culture, if we are embarrassed by such a God? Consequently, when we evangelize and share our faith, we tend to try to soften these harsh aspects of our God. But should we? Perhaps not! Here is the rest of the story:

> The apostles were performing many miraculous signs and wonders among the people. And all the believers were meeting regularly at the Temple in the area known as Solomon's Colonnade. But no one else dared to join them, even though all the people had high regard for them. Yet more and more people believed and were brought to the

Lord—crowds of both men and women. As a result of the apostles' work, sick people were brought … and they were all healed.

ACTS 5:12-16 NLT

Oddly, rather than discrediting the Church, *God's judgments were building the Church!*

~

We often wonder, "To what extent has the Church been taken captive by the culture of the West and its ideas?" Have judgment and justice gone out of style? Atheist Richard Dawkins, speaking for many of the educated in the West, famously claimed:

> The God of the Old Testament is arguably the most un-pleasant character in all fiction: jealous and proud of it; a petty, unjust, unforgiving control-freak; a vindictive, bloodthirsty ethnic cleanser; a misogynistic, homophobic, racist, infanticidal, genocidal, filicidal, pestilential, megalo-maniacal, sadomasochistic, capriciously malevolent bully.[1]

Although most Christians wouldn't go so far, we still find Dawkins' words stinging and embarrassing. We therefore tend to want to make excuses for His judgments. Some have even gone so far as to proclaim that God will save everyone. Some claim that God has repented of His harsh ways. Finally, some of us would like to be able to say that Ananias and Sapphira died because of a stricken conscience, and not from the judgment of God. But saying this would be misrepresenting God.

Understandably, we want others to be attracted to our God, so we do everything we can to massage His image and give Him a face-lift. However, what represents an improved image in our eyes is unacceptable to Him. Instead, His blessings accompany our faithful presentation, within the context of His love, of who He really is.

CHAPTER 19

Is the "Genocide"
of the Canaanites Unjust?

How do we answer the charge that is often made that the Old Testament God is a "beast"? Those who make this indictment usually start with God's command to destroy the Canaanites.

In *The Age of Reason*, Thomas Paine wrote, "Whenever we read the obscene stories ... the cruel and tortuous executions, the unrelenting vindictiveness with which ... the Bible is filled, it would be more consistent if we called it the work of a demon, than the word of God."[1]

Even those who consider themselves Christians are making this charge. Evolutionist and former co-head of the Biologos Foundation, Karl Giberson, made this amazing statement:

> "In *The God Delusion* [evolutionist and New Atheist Richard] Dawkins eloquently skewers the tyrannical anthropomorphic deity of the Old Testament—the God that supposedly commanded the Jews to go on genocidal rampages and who occasionally went on his own rampages, flooding the planet or raining fire and brimstone on wicked cities. But who believes in this deity any more, besides those same fundamentalists who think the earth is 10,000 years old? Modern theology has moved past this view of God."[2]

Many people of faith are embarrassed by these Old Testament portrayals of the God in whom they trust. It is therefore imperative that we try to make a defense for our God:

> ...but in your hearts honor Christ the Lord as holy, always being prepared to make a defense to anyone who asks you for a reason for the hope that is in you; yet do it with gentleness and respect.
>
> 1 PETER 3:15
> *see also Jude 3 and 2 Corinthians 10:4-5*

But how should we do this? I don't think that it is enough to simply say, "This world belongs to God. Therefore, He is perfectly free to do with it as He wishes." Although it is true that God, who has given us life, is perfectly justified to take life away at His good pleasure, this alone makes God seem unjust and uncaring. Yet we are impelled to admit that the artist is free to destroy his painting, whether he likes it or not. After all, it is his creation and belongs to him. However, a painting isn't the same as a human being.

Our God declares that He is holy and righteous. How do these attributes remain viable in regard to His order to destroy the Canaanites? Let me try to offer several points that we might consider:

The evil of the Canaanites was extensive.

In the *Christian Research Journal*, Clay Jones tries to justify God's judgments:

> The "new atheists" call God's commands to kill the Canaanites genocide, but a closer look at the horror of the Canaanites' sinfulness, exhibited in rampant idolatry, incest, adultery, child sacrifice, homosexuality, and bestiality, reveals that God's reason for commanding their death was not genocide but capital punishment.[3]

Indeed, God had nothing good to say about the Canaanites. Instead, He continually warned Israel against their practices:

> "Do not have sexual relations with your neighbor's wife and defile yourself with her. Do not give any of your children

to be sacrificed to Molech, for you must not profane the name of your God. I am the LORD. Do not lie with a man as one lies with a woman; that is detestable. Do not have sexual relations with an animal and defile yourself with it. A woman must not present herself to an animal to have sexual relations with it; that is a perversion. Do not defile yourselves in any of these ways, because this is how the nations that I am going to drive out before you became defiled."

LEVITICUS 18:20-24 NIV

Jones' own research agrees with the biblical assessment of the Canaanites:

Like the Ancient Near East (ANE) pantheons [of gods], the Canaanite pantheon was incestuous. Baal has sex with his mother Asherah, his sister Anat, and his daughter Pidray, and none of this is presented pejoratively ... There should be no surprise that bestiality would occur among the Canaanites, since their gods practiced it ... There were absolutely no prohibitions against bestiality in the rest of the ANE.[4]

If their gods were their role models, why should we surmise that the Canaanites would be motivated to rise, even an iota, above them, either sexually or according to any Old Testament moral measure? These revelations also support the Genesis 19 account of the entire male population of Sodom attempting to rape Lot's two male visitors. In Genesis 18, we are told that if God found just 10 righteous people in that town, He would not have destroyed it. Evidently, this miniscule "quorum" was not present. The deceiving and numbing power of sin is so powerful that when Lot tried to warn his "sons-in-law" regarding God's immanent destruction of Sodom, they thought he was "jesting," (Genesis 19:14). Evidently to them, Sodom wasn't such a bad place, and certainly not one which would warrant divine judgment. It was home! Indeed, our human tendency is often to become complacent, even in regard to the most blatant and destructive forms of criminality and aberrant behavior.

God warned the Canaanites and gave them ample time to repent.

However corrupted the Canaanites might have been at this point, God informed Abraham that He would give them an additional 400 years to repent and come to their senses. God's reason for this mercy and grace? " ... for the sin of the Amorites [Canaanites] has not yet reached its full measure" (Genesis 15:16). Despite all the miraculous evidence that this just and righteous God had shown Canaan and the surrounding nations, not one of them ever confessed and repented of their ways.

God had performed wondrous miracles in Egypt in order that " ... I might show you my power and that my name might be proclaimed in all the earth" (Exodus 9:16). And indeed, all the surrounding nations heard about the miracles that had taken place and the Israelite conquests that occurred before they entered the Promised Land. Yet, hearing of the hand of God moving so favorably concerning the Israelites did not lead the Canaanites to reassess their sinful lives or to confess their sins. Instead, they formed military alliances to resist the Israelite onslaught.

There was one prostitute in Jericho who did respond appropriately to the evidence. She and her family were subsequently rescued. Rahab confessed that:

> "We have heard how the LORD dried up the water of the Red Sea for you when you came out of Egypt, and what you did to Sihon and Og, the two kings of the Amorites east of the Jordan, whom you completely destroyed."
>
> JOSHUA 2:10

In light of all this, Clay Jones is right. God's judgment on the Canaanites was not a matter of genocide—it was capital punishment meted out to a hardened and unrepentant people. It was a matter of justice and not a matter of meanness. In fact, there is no account in the entire Bible of an individual or a people who sought God's forgiveness but were refused. Consequently, Rahab and her family were not only saved from the destruction of Jericho, but Rahab was honored as one of the progenitors of the coming Savior of the world.

God wanted to protect the innocent from corruption.

The God of Israel had an eminently valid reason for not waiting any longer to bring judgment upon the Canaanites. He moved decisively when He did, in order to protect the innocent from corruption:

> "Be careful not to make a treaty with those who live in the land; for when they prostitute themselves to their gods and sacrifice to them, they will invite you and you will eat their sacrifices. And when you choose some of their daughters as wives for your sons and those daughters prostitute themselves to their gods, they will lead your sons to do the same."
>
> EXODUS 34:15-16

Sadly, Israel didn't always take this danger seriously, even after seeing God's judgments. As a result, they brought upon themselves the same punishment for sin that the Canaanites experienced, just as God had warned:

> Again the Israelites did evil in the eyes of the LORD. They served the Baals and the Ashtoreths, and the gods of Aram, the gods of Sidon, the gods of Moab, the gods of the Ammonites and the gods of the Philistines. And because the Israelites forsook the LORD and no longer served him, he became angry with them. He sold them into the hands of the Philistines and the Ammonites.
>
> JUDGES 10:6-7

～

We cannot coherently judge God.

Generally, at this point, the atheist will complain that a real god wouldn't be so punitive, that human beings don't deserve such punishment. Yet, we cannot blame God for punishing because we too—in countries and cultures around the world—justly punish. How can we blame God for pronouncing judgment when we do the same thing through our legal system? Perhaps once we find a better way of dealing with murderers, kidnappers, and rapists, we can point an accusing finger at God. However, it seems that we are in desperate need of our courts, jails, and police. This is continually made painfully clear to us. When our police go on strike or are issued stand-down orders, brutality and crime explodes. Similarly, the reality and sometimes necessity of warfare is amply corroborated by human history. Wars will not go away through love, meditation, or by any other means. Nations need to be protected from other nations. The innocent need protection from oppressors.

There is also another reason why the skeptic scoffs at the judgments of God. Peter explains that the scoffers of his day "deliberately forget" about God's judgments (2 Peter 3:3-8; 2:4-9), sensing in them their own doom. They are willfully ignorant and choose to discount their moral culpability in several ways:

- They deny freewill;
- they claim that we are merely the products of nature and nurture;
- they claim that we need therapy, not punishment;
- they claim that the concepts of justice and morality are merely human inventions.

Nevertheless, they still know right from wrong because God has wired these truths into their minds and consciences. Consequently, when they bring indictments against the God of the Bible for His judgments, they are also indicting themselves. After all, they have been created in the moral likeness of God. Thus, they understand that a people can become so utterly sinful that they deserve judgment:

> Though they know God's righteous decree that those who practice such things deserve to die, they not only do them but give approval to those who practice them.
>
> ROMANS 1:32
> *see also Romans 2:14-16 and Romans 6:21*

However, those same people cannot live with the knowledge that they deserve judgment. So, they arm their consciences against this knowledge and become increasingly corrupt, even to the point of hating those who walk in God's light.

The morally relative skeptic is in a muddle. To bring charges against God, or against anyone else, he needs an absolute moral standard. It is exactly the same situation with a math teacher who needs absolutely correct answers in order to grade a test. However, the skeptic believes that right-and-wrong are just ideas that he has dreamed up. Therefore, if he is to live consistently with these beliefs, he cannot really bring his moral charges against anyone.

∽

In addition to the issues I have already raised, there is another problem with which we must deal. The Canaanites had babies who had not yet done evil. Doesn't their destruction violate God's claims that He is a just God? Perhaps not:

1. "How is justice served by killing an innocent infant?" We can respond to this query with another question: "Is justice truly served if God communicates to the Hitlers of this world that the implications of their crimes will not touch their children?" In fact, life itself teaches us that children have to suffer for the sins and follies of their parents (Numbers 14:33). This knowledge should make us more diligent to do right. As a probation officer for 15 years, many probationers would understandably tell me: "I now have a wife and children, and so I have to get my life together for their sake!" Perhaps it is according to the wisdom of God that our children's fate should be so closely tied to our own. Perhaps our understanding of justice is too truncated.

2. God has promised to lay upon the children the sins of the parents. Anyone can see the consequences of this promise. According to Exodus 34:7, we inherit the sins and weaknesses of our parents through an invisible process that we might liken to osmosis. Perhaps we will find that by unlocking the secrets of epigenetics, we will also find the mechanism of this transfer. For example, we already understand that our lifestyle induces changes to our epigenetics which will be passed on to our progeny. If this is the case, then it might follow that the Canaanite children have already been irreversibly tainted with the sins of their parents—sins that

would eventually corrupt Israel. If I may add a wonderful side note here, I don't think that this should now be a concern for Christians since, by coming to Christ, we and our children are cleansed from all unrighteousness (1 John 1:9; Titus 3:5; 1 Corinthians 7:14).

These are not concrete explanations for why God ordered the destruction of infants. I must admit that I don't fully understand; I am only offering possibilities. However, those who have learned to trust in our Lord trust Him enough to know that He will reconcile everything—justly and lovingly!

Finally, our Savior wouldn't be so punitive if there was no hope, no remedy for evil. One pastor, Carlton Pearson, claimed that he had turned away from the God of the Bible because He mistakenly believed that God lusted after the destruction of the wicked. Instead, the opposite is true:

> "As surely as I live, declares the Sovereign LORD, I take no pleasure in the death of the wicked, but rather that they turn from their ways and live. Turn! Turn from your evil ways! Why will you die, O house of Israel?"
>
> EZEKIEL 33:11

Whatever we have done, God welcomes us to confess our sins and to receive His forgiveness:

> "Come now, let us reason together, says the Lord: though your sins are like scarlet, they shall be as white as snow; though they are red like crimson, they shall become like wool. If you are willing and obedient, you shall eat the good of the land; but if you refuse and rebel, you shall be eaten by the sword; for the mouth of the Lord has spoken."
>
> ISAIAH 1:18–20
> *see also Leviticus 26:40–42*

Can We Truly Judge God?

Judging requires knowledge and the wisdom to apply that knowledge. Having wisdom compels us to recognize the limits of our knowledge. For example, I recognize that I do not have the knowledge to tell my dentist how to do his job. Instead, wisdom directs me to check the reviews and recommendations before I choose a dentist.

We might have great knowledge in one area, but pride can mislead us to believe that we also have great knowledge in other areas. Cornelius Hunter gives us an example:

> "The feeblest of designers," writes [evolutionist] Steve Jones, "could improve [the structure of the human eye]." This and other examples, says Jones, show that complex organs are "not the work of some great composer but of an insensible drudge: an instrument, like others, built by a tinkerer [the evolutionary process] rather than by a trained engineer."[1]

Jones admits that if the world is the product of blind evolution, then it should reflect the *imperfect* work of "the feeblest of designers." However, if the Designer of the world is the perfect, omnipotent and omniscient God, then His workmanship should reflect perfection.

Can we recognize perfection when we see it? Let us consider the human eye, whose design Jones so glibly disparages. If perfection is judged by what the eye can do—how it functions, repairs itself, and integrates harmoniously with the rest of the body's systems—we should be awestruck. The eye converts light waves into millions of chemical-electrical impulses, then sends them off to the brain in organized, instantaneous, sequential patterns. These patterns are then reconstructed by the mind, drawing upon memory and other modes of our learning, until the data can be recognized as something upon which we can make some sort of a decision. It is these visual impulses that enable us to make fine distinctions among a myriad of similar faces. They enable us to make thousands of precise decisions whenever we ride a bicycle or drive a car. This process, occurring millions of times each day in the life of a human being, goes far beyond what we can understand and anything that human technology could create. No mindless, chance process could hope to even approximate the marvels of the human eye.

When do our eyes mislead us? When do they give us incorrect data? Has anyone ever invented anything superior to the eye, offering to pluck out his eye and implant his own invention? Rather, let us compare our eye with what unintelligent natural forces fabricate. Have natural forces ever collaborated to produce anything of complexity and functionality? Has gravity ever written poetry? Has a hurricane ever recited Shakespeare, or called out your name? Has electricity ever painted your portrait, or told you, "I love you"? Have the tides ever written your name on the sand?

Instead, it can be persuasively argued that unintelligent forces have never produced an object with the appearance of intelligent design. For that to happen, it would be like throwing paint on a canvas and expecting the *Mona Lisa* to appear.

Does nature reflect the workmanship of the "feeblest of designers"—evolution? According to Cornelius Hunter, "bats map out objects as small as mosquitoes by sensing the echoes of their own squeaks." Such a skill could hardly be the workmanship of a "tinkerer!"

> [Fish] use underwater electric fields either passively or actively to sense objects around them including other fish. The details of such systems would fill books. Anyone familiar with today's sonar or radar systems knows the immense complexity inherent in such systems: the problems of sensing the echo in the presence of the

transmitted signal ... Yet the bat's detection abilities are superior to those of the best electronic sonar equipment.[2]

Then consider "the rattlesnake with heat-sensitive (infrared) sensors to image its prey at night."[3] Or consider the owl "with ears tuned to different frequencies, to better track its prey."[4] Somehow, these systems are perfect enough to keep their owners from going hungry. In fact, the evidence in favor of an intelligent Designer is so striking that:

> Amherst College astronomy professor George Greenstein (a pantheist or something similar), [writes], "As we survey all the evidence, the thought insistently arises that some supernatural agency, or rather Agency, must be involved. Is it possible that suddenly, without intending to, we have stumbled upon scientific proof of the existence of a Supreme Being? Was it God who stepped in and so providentially created the cosmos for our benefit?"[5]

Do these wonders represent evidence of perfection and a Supreme Designer? If their design and construction represent more than just chance, then the only candidate left standing is God. Can the skeptical judge build a case against ID [Intelligent Design]? Steven Jones has claimed that the human eye is so flawed that natural random causation could easily explain it. But can random causation explain anything? Even if he could assemble from scratch something better than the human eye—along with a mind that could accurately interpret and reconstruct its millions of impulses each moment—Jones faces many other obstacles:

- He would have to prove that his creation does not have hidden costs. For instance, would his creation undermine other connected systems? What about other long-range costs or tradeoffs?
- He would have to demonstrate that mindless forces—if they exist—could construct and assemble structures like his creation.

What does all this have to do with the challenges against God's righteousness? There are many who claim that if God is all-powerful and all-loving, He should have created us without the possibility of suffering and death. But what would be the hidden costs, the long-range consequences, if there were beings who lived timelessly and without suffering?

Is it possible that the absence of death and pain might negatively impact God's blessed plan for humanity? We would be like lepers who cannot experience pain but end up suffering the consequences further down the road. How could the skeptic investigate those consequences? To judge God, he would have to have knowledge of the big picture of eternity. Perhaps suffering and death are necessary to prepare us for eternity:

> So we do not lose heart. Though our outer self is wasting away, our inner self is being renewed day by day. For this light momentary affliction is preparing for us an eternal weight of glory beyond all comparison.
>
> 2 CORINTHIANS 4:16–17

Can the skeptic discount this? No! We lack knowledge of the big picture, apart from the little that the Bible reveals. Therefore, once again, if the skeptic is going to bring any valid charges against God, he would need to see the big picture—eternity! Consequently, Jones is like the 1st-grader who wrongly judges his teacher for not teaching math correctly. If the student lacks the necessary knowledge to bring a cogent charge against his teacher, perhaps we are in the same situation when we attempt to discount God's righteousness.

However, we cannot leave our analysis at this point since the skeptic will ask:

> *Well, if you admit that you cannot judge God, what basis do you have to believe in your God?*

Admittedly, there is much that goes beyond our understanding. However, there is much that we do understand. Perhaps we should be like children who, although they do not understand their parents' plans, they have experienced and know the love and care of their parents, so they trust them.

Jesus has proved Himself to me in many ways. He has purchased me with His own blood, and I am thrilled to belong to Him and to serve Him with every fiber of my being.

APPENDIX

Why Do We Hate the God of the Bible
and Seek to Malign Him?

We often hate the things that are closest to us: Christianity, Western Civilization, capitalism, and even the principles that had once made the West great.

Why is this? These foundational elements of our culture provide the metrics by which we judge ourselves. And if we feel judged—and to some degree all of us feel judged—we hate the source of those judgments.

For instance, capitalism represents the requirement that we succeed, along with the concurrent threat of failure if we don't. Christianity represents the accusing finger which points out that we have failed to maintain its moral standards. We even resent our parents when we feel that we have failed to live up to their standards, especially when those standards interfere with what we want. Sometimes this resentment can turn into hatred.

I too had once been a hater. Perhaps this hatred of all that had made the West great helps to explain our attraction to counter-cultural elements, which, from a safe distance, seem to be comfortable alternatives.

Before Charles Manson had moved to Los Angeles, where he would collect the band of "disciples" who would murder on his behalf, he stayed with my college roommate Bob and me in Berkeley, California. Bob had met Charlie on the Berkeley campus one night during an impromptu jam session. Bob played his guitar and Charlie found a can for his drum. When they quit playing, Charlie asked Bob, "Do you have a place where I can crash?" We had a couch in our living room, and so Bob invited him back.

Charlie was a talker, and we were glad to listen. He seemed to be quite "evolved," so we thought he was cool. He talked about dropping acid and dancing with the energy of the surrounding trees—and killing cops. But comments like that weren't a problem for us. In fact, that was the sort of thing that all the "Woke" were talking about. We listened with enthusiasm to all he had to say. He never showed any interest in us or in what we were thinking, but why should he?

We never thought of him as being deranged in any way. In fact, one night Bob slipped into my room to ask, with excitement in his voice: "Who does Charlie remind you of?" I told him I didn't know. Almost gushing, Bob asked me, "Doesn't he remind you of Jesus Christ?" Annoyed, I answered, "Bob, I'm Jewish, and Jesus doesn't trigger any image for me."

Why were we not able to see Charlie for the psychopath that he was? How was it that his group of women—who accepted him as a Christ figure—were unable to see the disconnect? We were possessed with the zeitgeist of the sixties, and the past and its lessons were no longer relevant for us. Therefore, we were receptive to the approaching new age where love and peace would reign. We were eager to reject the ancient repressive restrictions of Christianity in favor of the Age of Aquarius and free love. The choice was easy.

~

How was Adolph Hitler able to take control of the minds of perhaps the most highly educated nation in the world, thus proving that even "education" is no defense against the insanity of our age? How did the cult leader, Jim Jones, succeed in luring almost 1000 of his followers to commit suicide? How could the Manson girls have been so blinded and deceived that they could stab their innocent victims to death? Is it possible that we too could be similarly blinded by our social context?

Even now, educated Westerners are celebrating many failed lifestyles and philosophies—Shariah Law, Marxism, polyamory—whatever might give them the hope of acceptance, significance, value, love, joy, and peace. In other words, they are celebrating and lionizing anything that will offer them freedom from feeling judged. A friend of mine who wholeheartedly embraces this mind-set has opted for the belief that he lacks the freedom to act contrary to his own self-aggrandizement. In this way, he is able to minimize any feelings of guilt or shame for anything he chooses to do.

In a way, my friend's stance makes sense, doesn't it? We all need to bathe our faults and failures in the waters of some sort of forgiveness. And this is the very thing that Christ offers us:

> If we say we have no sin, we deceive ourselves, and the truth is not in us. If we confess our sins, he is faithful and just to forgive us our sins and to cleanse us from all unrighteousness.
>
> 1 JOHN 1:8–9

This Faith has been the cornerstone of Western civilization, including the many benefits we have long enjoyed. It has provided the answer to our deepest need—the love of God:

> … but God shows his love for us in that while we were still sinners, Christ died for us. Since, therefore, we have now been justified by his blood, much more shall we be saved by him from the wrath of God. For if while we were enemies we were reconciled to God by the death of his Son, much more, now that we are reconciled, shall we be saved by his life.
>
> ROMANS 5:8–10

This Truth assures us of God's love—even for the most undeserving. It is with this assurance that we can begin to live at peace with, and accept, ourselves.

However, could this be no more than the grandest of all delusions? I had long struggled with this doubt. As a result, all of the questions I have raised in this book have been quite real for me. They were, in a very tangible sense, demons from which I could not escape. Instead, I found myself compelled to face them. Although I have not been able to provide my doubts with *comprehensive* answers, Christ has been able to give me what I have needed to silence their roar.

Why the God of the Bible?

Even if this book has succeeded in at least neutralizing the charges that the God of the Bible is evil, there remains the question: "Why do you believe that it was the God of the Bible who created everything? Perhaps, instead, it had been another god, or other gods." A skeptic might offer this challenge:

> *Even if you are correct and all scientific and "naturalist" explanations eventually lead back to a supernatural accounting, you have absolutely no basis to determine which supernatural explanation is the actual truth. All you have is a book that says, "This is the truth," among a million other books claiming the same thing but with completely different explanations.*

In response, I think that the evidence best fits the biblical description of the biblical God. In the same way that a book requires an author, the universe requires a competent Creator. Furthermore, this Creator must have all of the following characteristics.

Eternal and Uncaused

How do we account for anything? There must be a sufficient, uncaused Causer—who doesn't require a prior cause—from whom all else originated. In fact, causation makes no sense without an uncaused, eternal Causer. Without such a God, there is nothing that possesses an adequate cause or explanation. If instead, the universe was eternal and uncaused, there could never be a rational explanation for anything. Why? Because everything would require a prior cause—which would lead to an illogical, infinite regress of causation.

Besides, if time is infinite and eternal, it would be impossible for an infinite number of years to ever arrive in the present.

In addition, only an uncaused Causer is capable of accounting for how this world of molecules-in-motion is maintained. For one thing, the immutable and universal laws of science would need a transcendent explanation if everything else in the universe is in constant flux.

Omnipotent

The cause must always be greater than the effect. To create and then to harmoniously hold all things together—including the immutable and elegant laws of science—requires an all-powerful God. There are many realities that depend on an omnipotent God: existence, freewill, consciousness, objective moral truth, life, DNA, the immutable laws of science, answers to prayer, and the fine-tuning of the universe, to name just a few.

Omniscient

The world requires the design and harmony that can only come from omniscience. We have no evidence of a god tampering with the laws of science, trying to improve any mistakes. It seems that, instead, God had an adequate understanding of what He was doing from the very beginning. This interpretation also puts the kibosh on the possibility that there are multiple, necessarily finite, gods. Such a panoply of gods would be unable to account for the stability of the universe and its laws. Multiple gods would also defy the principle of parsimony, also known as Occam's Razor, which requires the simplest explanation. A theory that requires many parts also requires many leaps of faith, and the more such leaps are required, the less probable the theory. The biblical understanding of God provides the simplest, most sensible, and satisfying explanation of how the world was created and how it continues to be maintained.

Righteous

Because we were all created in the image of God, the fact that God is righteous explains our desire and willingness to do the right thing, even when our emotions tell us to run. A righteous God provides the only possible basis for objective moral truth and meaning, the things that our hearts crave. Otherwise, society would be a competition between many different wills and ideas, all trying to dominate the others through raw force.

Besides, if our Creator is evil, there would be no reason to be good. Rather, any attempt at goodness might infuriate him. Instead, the moral laws inscribed upon our conscience tend to accord with those of the God of the Bible.

Just

In a world without an omniscient and supremely moral God of justice, society would need to invent just laws to maintain order. Parents would still need to teach their children the difference between right and wrong, good and bad, and just and unjust. In that process, those same parents would be playing "make-believe" with their kids, teaching them that these non-existent entities of right and wrong have some sort of authority over their lives. In the same way, teachers would need to play make-believe and instruct their students that it is wrong to bully and to cheat. Any laws enacted in such a society would be no more than reflections of the evolving social conventions of those in power.

Once the God of the Bible is rejected, people would have to live disingenuously in many other areas of life. People would have to imagine that all of the following could exist without believing in God: freewill, human responsibility, honor, meaning, equality, human rights, and integrity.

One

The harmony and immutability we find in science is best accounted for by the existence of a single God, rather than in a competition among many gods, which would create insurmountable disorder.

Love

Creation as we know it seems to be incredibly fine-tuned to fulfill our desires and needs. It satisfies all of our longings for food, drink, family, friendship, sex, and aesthetics—all in a way that shows us that the Creator loves us. God's miraculous answers to our prayers also confirm His love for us. In addition, His love will eventually satisfy the rest of our needs in His promised heaven.

Truth

God is the one sought-after unifying principle or cause. God's truth satisfies our need to know and systematically understand how all knowledge fits together. Even our planet seems to be precisely situated in a place that maximizes knowability. Consequently, truth is not only knowable but elegant. Just look at the precise and elegant laws that make science and learning possible!

∾

All the above suggests that the creation, including ourselves, is the product of no less a god than the God of the Bible. No other Source can better explain the reality that we navigate—even our own psychology—than the God of the Bible.

Besides everything that I have mentioned in this chapter, there are many reasons to believe that the Bible is divinely authored: The miracles of the Bible, fulfilled prophecies, biblical wisdom which has changed lives and elevated Bible-centered cultures, and internal and external supportive evidence. We need to remember these truths. Consequently, Moses continually reminded Israel of all the multiple reasons they had to trust in their God:

> … you shall not be afraid of them but you shall remember what the LORD your God did to Pharaoh and to all Egypt, the great trials that your eyes saw, the signs, the wonders, the mighty hand, and the outstretched arm, by which the LORD your God brought you out. So will the LORD your God do to all the peoples of whom you are afraid.
>
> DEUTERONOMY 7:18–19

Fear can control our lives. Therefore, we must remember our God, who can empower us! It is only when we recall His truth that we are enabled to stand against adversity and threat.

BIBLIOGRAPHY

INTRODUCTION

1. Dawkins, Richard. *The God Delusion.* 1st ed., Mariner Books, 2006, p. 31.

CHAPTER 1

1. *"The Lesson of the Butterfly."* Paulo Coelho, 11 July 2008, paulocoelhoblog.com/2007/12/10/the-lesson-of-the-butterfly.

CHAPTER 2

1. *"Original Sin"* OrthodoxWiki, 4 Mar. 2010, orthodoxwiki.org/Original_sin.

2. Kuchar, Philip. "The Incoherence of Original Sin and Substitutive Sacrifice" Internet Infidels, 17 Sept. 2021, https://infidels.org/kiosk/article/the-incoherence-of-original-sin-and-substitutive-sacrifice/.

CHAPTER 5

1. http://www.youtube.com/watch?v=pwGLNbiw1gk
"Video unavailable. This video is no longer available because the YouTube account associated with this video has been terminated."

2. Nagel, Thomas. *The Last Word,* 1st ed., Oxford University Press, 1997, p. 130.

CHAPTER 6

1. Jones, Tony. *Jesus' Death, God's Culpability.* Theoblogy, 12 Sept. 2014, www.patheos.com/blogs/tonyjones/2014/09/12/jesus-death-gods-culpability.

CHAPTER 8

1. Ingersoll, Robert Green. "A Christmas Sermon." *The Works of Robert G. Ingersoll,* edited by C. P. Farrell, vol. 7, New York, The Dresden Publishing Co., 1902, p. 268.

2. Karl Giberson, *Exposing the Straw Men of New Atheism,* BioLogos. org, Part 5 (October 25, 2010).

3. Lewis, C. S. *Mere Christianity.* New York, Macmillan Publising Company, 1960, p. 31.

4. Volf, Miroslav. *Exclusion and Embrace: A Theological Exploration of Identity, Otherness, and Reconciliation.* Nashville, Abingdon Press, 1996, pp. 303-304.

5. Keller, Timothy. *The Reason for God: Belief in an Age of Skepticism,* Boston, Dutton, 2008, p. 75.

6. Ibid., 78

7. Lewis, C. S. *The Great Divorce.* New York, Macmillan Publising Company, 1978, pp. 78-79.

8. Ibid., p. 79.

CHAPTER 9

1. Graffagnino, Tom. *No Border Land: Finding Amazing Grace in a Dark and Dying World,* Grand Rapids, Credo House Publishers, 2020, p. 167.

2. Horton, Michael. *Christless Christianity: The Alternative Gospel of the American Church,* Ada, Michigan, Baker Books, 2012, p. 104.

CHAPTER 13

1. Mangalwadi, Vishal. *The Book That Made Your World: How the Bible Created the Soul of Western Civilization*, Nashville, Thomas Nelson, 2012, p. 114.

2. D'Souza, Dinesh. *What's So Great About Christianity* Washington, D.C., Salem Books, 2007, p. 73.

3. Ibid., p. 75.

CHAPTER 14

1. Jaffa, Harry V. "Homosexuality and the Natural Law." Center for the Study of the Natural Law, Claremont Institute, 1990, pp. 3-4.

CHAPTER 16

1. Atterton, Peter. "A God Problem." *The New York Times*, 25 Mar. 2019, www.nytimes.com/2019/03/25/opinion/-philosophy-god-omniscience.html.

2. Ibid.

3. Ibid.

4. Ibid.

5. Ibid.

6. Ibid.

CHAPTER 17

1. Durant, Will and Ariel Durant. *The Lessons of History*. Manhattan, New York City, Simon and Schuster, 1968, p. 93.

CHAPTER 18

1. Dawkins, Richard. *The God Delusion*. 1st ed., Mariner Books, 2006, p. 31.

CHAPTER 19

1. Paine, Thomas. *The Age of Reason*, 1795, London, H. D. Symonds.

2. Giberson, Karl. *Exposing the Straw Men of New Atheism*, BioLogos. org, Part 5 (October 25, 2010).

3. Jones, Clay. "Killing the Canaanites: A Response to the New Atheism's 'Divine Genocide' Claims." *Christian Research Journal*, vol. 33, no. 4, 1994, p. 31.

4. Ibid., p. 31.

CONCLUSION

1. Hunter, Cornelius. *Darwin's God: Evolution and the Problem of Evil*. Eugene, Oregon, Wipf and Stock Publishers, 2019, p. 83.

2. Ibid.

3. Ibid.

4. Ibid., p. 72

5. Schaefer, Henry, et al. *Science and Christianity: Conflict or Coherence?*, 2016, The Apollos Trust, 2016, p. 62.

*

www.ingramcontent.com/pod-product-compliance
Lightning Source LLC
Chambersburg PA
CBHW061822040426
42447CB00012B/2763